Dear Mom

ROBIN & DOUG WEBSTER

A JANET THOMA BOOK

THOMAS NELSON PUBLISHERS
Nashville • Atlanta • London • Vancouver
Printed in the United States of America

Published in Nashville, Tennessee, by Thomas Nelson, Inc., Publishers, and distributed in Canada by Word Communications, Ltd., Richmond, British Columbia.

The Bible version used in this publication is THE NEW KING JAMES VERSION. Copyright © 1979, 1980, 1982, 1990 Thomas Nelson, Inc., Publishers.

The research for this book was conducted among 1,000 children and adults across the United States. To protect the privacy of individuals who are quoted or referenced in his book, all names and certain identifying details have been changed. No reference to any person, living or dead, is intended and any use of the names of actual persons is purely coincidental. While true names and specific details have been changed, the meaning has been preserved.

ISBN 0- 7852-7589-4

Printed in the United States of America.

1 2 3 4 5 6 — 01 00 99 98 97 96

To a pair of ladies who went through their own labor of love to birth and raise the authors of Dear Mom, Myrna Glick (Robin's mom) and Patricia Kowalski (Doug's mom).

Special thanks to some incredible ladies we call friends who model what it means to be a mom: Sherri Alden, Cathy Burns, Jana Burwell, Kim Carpenter, Charlotte Dean, Melinda Douros, Lynette Fisher, Christa Kelso, Lori Marshall, Laurie Pilz, and Debbie Webster.

CONTENTS

ACKNOWLEDGMENTS

Like birthing and raising children, book writing is never a solo flight. You don't see their names on the cover of the book, but the influence of some wonderful people is spread throughout the inside pages. We would like to thank the following people for their valuable and gifted contribution to Dear Mom:

Shirley Webster for guiding Doug through his teenage years as his stepmom.

Janet Thoma for investing her expertise as an editor and a mom.

The unsung partners at Thomas Nelson Publishers for extending hope to many moms.

Sealy, Susan and Tom of Team Yates for believing in the Websters' desire to make a difference in the lives of kids and their families.

Laurie Pilz and Maryanne Pilz who served as partners in this book by translating the priceless input from young people.

The women of Coast Hills Church's MOPS group who allow Robin to share the journey of motherhood with them.

The youth workers and teachers who helped us hear the hearts of young people.

PART
ONE

If I could tell you anything . . .

WHAT KIDS SAY . . .

"You're the greatest mom in the world."

"Thanks for sacrificing so much to raise me."

WHAT KIDS MEAN . . .

I love you and I appreciate
what you have done for me.

WHAT KIDS NEED . . .

Women who want to leave a legacy of love for their children.

CHAPTER 1

> *Dear Mom,*
>
> *Thank you for your labor of love.*
>
> *Love,*
> *Your child*

A LABOR OF LOVE

My mom is the color brown. I have the utmost respect for her. Brown is a dignified color.

Dan, seventeen years old

My mom is the color lavender; it's a pretty color and there is nothing like it.

Sterling, thirteen and one-half years old

Mom, sometimes you get a little rambunctious. Most of the time you are the best.

Mike, fifteen years old

R obin remembers all too well the day she first became a mom, as many moms probably do:

"The contractions started after dinner one evening in early November, 1986. The hours passed slowly. By the time we hit the road for the hospital, it was the middle of the night so we avoided the usual California bumper-to-bumper traffic.

"We entered the hospital educated with all the latest and greatest breathing techniques, none of which Doug used. Our hopes for an immediate arrival and an early departure were not in our baby's plans. Brookelyn took her time—all of the night and the morning that followed. What I experienced that night has become commonplace for so many moms: intermittent sleep. During my pregnancy people complimented me for "that glow." Ten years and three kids later, I am still trying to recapture it. The best remedy I have found is to apply the product called White Out under my eyes. Maybe wearing a veil would be more effective!

"In spite of the pain, the months of indigestion, the expansion of my skin to sizes unknown in my former life, the swollen ankles and enough water retention to irrigate Death Valley, I forgot everything when they placed the wonderful pink bundle of baby Webster in my arms. I cried. Doug cried. Our baby cried. Then our baby cried more. And when all that was done, our baby continued to cry. One nurse offered these consoling words, 'Oh, Mrs. Webster, your baby has a good set of lungs.'"

Of course, Doug, as the dad, remembers the event a little differently.

DOUG'S VERSION OF THE BLESSED EVENT

"I was ready to do whatever I needed to help Robin through a very rough go—bringing a little baby with a big head into a huge world through a very small opening. I knew pain would be associated with that experience. Fortunately, I was a certified coach, a bona fide graduate of a Lamaze course, so I was prepared like a Boy Scout on his first camping trip.

"I had heard about women being struck by contractions and finding themselves thrust into a stratosphere of pain, which inspired them to explode emotionally like a rocket from a launch pad. I had been told that labor and delivery rooms make divorce court seem mild by comparison. I did not know what to expect, but I was ready.

"The contractions were getting stronger and closer as we drove to the hospital that night. Fortunately for me and my reputation as a man and a husband, Robin chose not to destroy me verbally or dismember me physically. She went inward with her pain. I watched her curl up on the front seat of the van. I knew what was happening. (Remember, I was a certified coach.)

"The Lamaze teacher told us coaches that the gentle touch of another person can be a soothing anesthesia for women in labor, plus it may release endorphins to help the mother with the pain. I placed my hand ever so gently on Robin's left knee and proceeded to rub her leg, thinking, *Come on endorphins, do your thing!*

"Without looking up, Robin reached from her fetal position, grasped my hand, and held it in her hand. I thought to myself, *It really works! All those nights we wasted lying on a floor equipped with a pillow while listening to a nurse speak of the marvels of pregnancy and the mystery of birth are now paying off. Even the time she asked the pregnant women to pinch their leg of their coaches so they would empathize with the mom's pain seemed okay.*

"And then it happened. Without a word, Robin ever so gently took my hand from her leg and placed it back on my leg. Somehow I knew my beautiful wife, the woman who was about to give me the greatest gift, was delivering one silent but clear message, 'Touch me again, mister, and you'll have to learn how to live without one hand.' I got the point. Then and there, endorphins or not, I moved from being coach to cheerleader. I learned to sit back out of arms reach and encourage."

As you know firsthand, being a mom is not an easy task. Years ago a friend of ours showed us the card he was sending to his mom for Mother's Day. The cover read: "Mom, you should have known raising me would be a tough job." The inside of the card stated: "When I made you throw up before I was even born."

Being a mom is a labor of love. Unfortunately, this does not end in the delivery room. The labor, the pain, the confusion, and the postpartum continue long after the doctor's bills have been paid. Mom's role is a revolving account with a balance due month after month. Motherhood has never been easy.

Add to this historic challenge the difficulty of raising a child in today's culture, and you have yourself a near-impossible endeavor.

Yet the sacrifice often pays off in spades.

THE SACRIFICE OF MOTHERHOOD BEHIND THE SUCCESS OF A MAN

One of the most successful and respected business leaders of our time is Lee Iacocca. If you ever owned a Chrysler or Ford, you have probably received the benefit of his professional expertise. In his autobiography, he offers a touching testimonial to his mom. He writes:

Economically, our family had its ups and downs. Like many Americans, we did well during the 1920s. My father started making lots of money in real estate, in addition to his other businesses. For a few years we were actually wealthy. But then came the Depression. No one who has lived through it can ever forget. My father lost all his money.

During those difficult years, my mother was very resourceful. She was a real immigrant mother, the backbone of the family. A nickel soupbone went a long way in our house, and we always had enough to eat. I remember that she used to buy squabs—three birds for a quarter—and kill the birds herself because she didn't trust the butcher to guarantee their freshness. As the Depression grew worse, she helped out in my father's restaurant. At one point she went to work in a silk mill, sewing shirts. Whatever it took to keep going, she did it gladly. Today she's still a beautiful woman—who looks younger than I do.[1]

What stood behind Iacocca? A sacrificial mom. What stood behind Mrs. Iacocca and her family? Lee writes, "Like so many in those days, our strong belief in God sustained us."[2]

Few of our children will write an autobiography as a tribute to us. More realistically, only a handful will take the time to let the world know what their mom did for them. How unfortunate. There is good news, however. The message of love and gratitude toward mom, although often silent, is abundant in the hearts of our children. This book is a child's rallying cry for mom. Throughout these pages you will find what kids want their moms to know if they could tell them anything.

DEAR MOM, IF I COULD TELL YOU ANYTHING . . .

This book is not comprised of one woman's or one man's opinions. The content of *Dear Mom* comes from one thousand young people and adults who participated in written surveys, face-to-face interviews, or counseling sessions. These personal encounters are part of the thirty cumulative years we've worked with young people and moms.

Although we have three kids of our own and have spent numerous years working with young people and families, we are not parenting experts. Robin has not earned a Masters in Motherhood, and Doug doesn't hold a Ph.D. in Daddiology. The three Webster children take up enough of Robin's time to shortcut her pursuit of "Expert Mother" status. She is too busy being a mom to be an expert on motherhood.

Instead we worked diligently to find out what it means to be good moms, according to the ones who know best: the kids who live with them. Our survey was simple in structure to provide the greatest amount of participation. We asked three open-ended questions:

1. If I were to describe my mom with a color, she would be _____ because . . .

2. If I were to rate my relationship with my mom on a scale of one to ten (ten being the highest), mine would be a _____ because . . .

3. If I could say anything to my mom, I would tell her . . .

Although the answers did not catch us off guard, the intensity and emotion of the responses did. A few were so strong in language and tone, our seasoned team at Thomas Nelson Publishing advised us to leave them out to avoid offense. As we read kids' comments about their moms, we were tossed like a boat on a sea of hope and fear, guilt and pride, confusion and confirmation. Our discovery from this journey consists of nine key messages young people want their moms to know. Each of the nine messages fell under one of three major themes:

Theme 1: Cheers of the Heart
Theme 2: Tears of the Heart
Theme 3: Celebration of Mom

The first theme, Cheers of the Heart, is described with four positive messages:

- Mom, you're always there.
- I can tell you anything.
- We get along.
- You're a fun mom.

We also found four equally poignant messages describing the second theme, Tears of the Heart:

- Mom, you're *always* there!
- I can't tell you anything.
- Quit yelling and chill out!
- I could live without you.

You have probably noticed that these heart-felt feelings of children are the negative side to the four Cheers of the Heart.

Dear Mom's ninth and final message stands alone as it contributes to the heart and soul of the third theme, Celebration of Mom:

- I love you and I appreciate everything you've done for me.

Have you ever wondered, "Does my child notice and appreciate everything I do?" When you finish the final message, you'll be convinced your effort is well spent.

We asked one fifteen-year-old young man to rate his relationship with his mom on a scale of one to ten. He gave it a seven. Although it was not what it could be, Thao recognized this one powerful factor in the relationship. He said:

She is willing to do anything and lose a lot of things in life just for me.

In other words, Thao's mom made many sacrifices for her son. Thao was not alone. Sixteen-year-old Kim told us about her mom. If she could say anything to her mom, Kim wants her mom to know this:

I love you, Mom. Thanks for sacrificing yourself and giving me the best life possible.

At age sixteen, Mitch is well aware of the priority his mom places on him, often putting him before herself. He says his mom is like the color white because . . .

She is so generous and kind. She never puts herself before anyone.

When it comes to kids' response to mom's sacrifice, many of them want to celebrate mom on more than just one holiday each year. When we asked, we heard hundreds of kids saying, *Mom, I love you and thanks for everything you've done for me.*

Some of them even go as far as saying, *Mom, you're the best!* We'll let them speak for themselves.

> *There's no mom that's better.*
> Melissa, fifteen years old

Krista begs to differ with Melissa. Krista thinks there is a better mom than Melissa's and it's Krista's. She gives her mom the number one status in the world.

> *Mom, you're the greatest person in the world.*
> Krista, fourteen years old

"Why settle for just planet Earth?" Jennifer asks herself. When it comes to Jennifer's mom, she's out of this world.

She's the best mom in the whole universe. I love her sooooo much.
Jennifer, eleven years old

Not to be outdone by Melissa, Krista, and Jennifer, Bonny takes the "Best Mom" competition to a new level.

My mom is better than the best Mom.
Bonny, twelve years old

And that's not all. We have more young people who want to line up for the best mom. Let us drop a few names:

Bryn, Ciara, Jennifer, Mike, Kassandra, Rebekah

Mom, the good news is your child may want to join the competition and give you the top honors!

One young man named Dan does not want to compete in the "Who's the Best Mom Pageant." (He may be wise. Melissa, Krista, Jennifer, and Bonny sound like serious competitors.) He paints his mom a rich brown color when he describes her.

My mom is the color brown. I have the utmost respect for her. Brown is a dignified color.
Dan, seventeen years old

In case you are wondering if the kids we found live in a fairy tale land run by a Cinderella mom, listen to what Mike has to say:

Sometimes she gets a little rambunctious. Most of the time she is the best.

Mike, fourteen years old

Some children are not as fortunate as Mike, Jennifer, and the rest of the "Best Mom" bunch. One seventeen-year-old young person refused to offer his or her name, but told us:

Our relationship is a zero. She is bad. I could live without her.

If you fear you may be on the receiving end of some painful comments from your child, read on. Your relationship with your child may be more labor than love, but there is hope. Healing can happen between a mother and child.

Mom, the courage, commitment, and compassion of the young people we bring to you may be the very strength you need to hang in there. Don't just listen to us. Hear some of our young friends who have a powerful cry of the heart, such as one seventeen-year-old young man:

I usually feel distant, yet I do encounter close moments that I wish there were more of.

I wish there were more close moments with my mom, he says. Why? You, Mom, are the one person kids want to encounter in a very close, loving way. Your effort from the drive to the hospital to the day you picked up *Dear Mom* are worth it. Your children and our world will be better because of it. Behind every success is a woman, likely a mom, making a difference through a labor of love.

Our purpose in offering you *Dear Mom* is to give you an

inside look at your child's heart so you can draw closer to your child, whatever his or her age. Each chapter includes a section called "What's a Mother to Do?," which provides practical suggestions to deal with each of the nine messages from kids.

Dear Mom is a book of pondering the hearts of young people as they talked about their moms. Let's open our *own* hearts to hear what they have to share with us.

Dear Mom,

I am grateful for all the sacrifices you've made to bring me into this world and raise me.

Love,
Your child

PART
TWO

TALK
FROM THE
HEART:

Cheers and Tears

WHAT KIDS SAY . . .

"We've been through a lot together and you're always there for me."

"Relax and don't worry, even if it is your job."

"I love being with you, Mom, and I can share anything with you."

WHAT KIDS MEAN . . .

I am grateful for you, mom.

Don't control my life.

*I really enjoy my relationship
with you, Mom*

WHAT KIDS NEED . . .

Self-controlled moms who trust their children.

Moms who hear the heart of their children.

*Moms who have a hopeful, purposeful, fun
out look on life.*

CHAPTER 2

> *Dear Mom,*
>
> *You're*
> *always there.*
>
> *Love,*
> *Your child*

MOM, YOU'RE ALWAYS THERE.

Though she's not perfect she's always been there for me and taught me how to be strong.

Susan, nineteen years old

I chose the brightest color there is—yellow, because it reminds me of the sun. My mom is always there. Those days the clouds come in, she's always missed.

Virginia, fifteen years old

Thank you for coming out and watching every game I play in.

Michael, sixteen years old

Her dark hair flows loosely down and around her smooth face to lay in soft large waves on her shoulders. Her eyes are endearing but commanding, enticing yet confident. Her face features a narrow nose accented by a strong jaw line. Luscious lips separate the two. She was recently voted one of the fifty most beautiful people in the world by People magazine. Believe us, you'd hate her from the moment you saw her.

Who is she? She is a mom, just like you. Now, I'll bet you feel even more inadequate. She is also the lead character, Devon Adair, portrayed by Debrah Farentino on the television show *Earth 2*. Devon is what some critics are calling the new generation of "She TV" or the "She Pack." She is one of the new breed of leading ladies, including Captain Kathryn Janeway, the first female commander of a Star Trek spaceship, and Sydney Bloom, in *VR5* goes where women normally won't go as she travels into other people's head via virtual reality goggles and gloves.

On *Earth 2* Devon is stubborn yet sensitive. Janeway, in Star Trek, is commanding yet caring. In *VR5* Bloom is fearless yet feminine.

Debrah Farentino, age thirty-five, who plays Devon Adair, was six months pregnant with her second child while filming the finale for the '95 season. (How would you like to be filmed six months into your second pregnancy? Sometimes pregnant women don't even want to leave the house, let alone go public for millions to see.) Television character Adair is described by one critic as, "The most stubborn, most kind, and most persistent of them all, and her white T-shirt hasn't gotten dirty yet."[1]

Mom, your job is tough enough. Now you have to compete with cosmic queens who are out of this world in strength, character, courage, and looks. Face facts, Mom, the new breed of female heroes are mostly gorgeous and young. (With rare exceptions, such as Angela Lansbury of *Murder She Wrote*.) These shows definitely push social boundaries to open new dialogue about the role of women in today's society.

Although many of these heroines are single (television is struggling to match career and motherhood), Devon of *Earth 2* is driven by a powerful motive called *motherhood*. She is driven to explore places unknown in search of earthlike air for her sick son.

Bottom line for *Earth 2,* a show with an unknown future on the tube but a forceful image in our society: motherhood matters. Even the single women of the Tech and Trek variety seem remarkably nurturing. Somehow these women can champion compassion while commanding as captain of the ship. Television has come a long way since the era of Donna Reed, *Father Knows Best,* and the maid on *Hazel.* But through it all, the maternal side of the feminine nature is still present.

Mom, rest assured. You do not have to strap yourself in the captain's seat or pull on your virtual reality gloves to leave a lasting impact on our world. When we spent time listening to a thousand young people talk about you, real moms in our present day world, they did not talk about television heroines. They spoke of you: everyday moms who raise their kids each day of each year of their childhood.

MOM, IF I COULD TELL YOU ANYTHING . . .

One of the strongest messages that came across the airwaves from kids to moms was this positive, powerful statement, *Mom, you're always there.*

Listen to what the young people say about their moms:

> *Our relationship is always there for me to lean on.*
> Hannah, sixteen years old

We are always there for each other, and we have both been through a lot together.

Nick, fourteen years old

She always listens to what I have to say, is always there for me, no matter what.

Jessica, thirteen years old

Mom, you're always there is the first message in what we call the Cheers of the Heart, four positive messages from kids. At a young age your child knows that your presence in his or her life provides the foundation from which he or she can grow, and that you provide a home to which he or she can return. Mom, time and time again we heard kids say in one fashion or another, you're always there. What do they mean by that statement? Let us offer four blessings on kids whose moms are always there.

1. The Blessing of Security

A young woman named Susan offered the ideal comment for moms who are far from flawless but committed to their children. On a scale of one to ten, Susan gave her relationship with her mom an eight. Why so high? Susan told us:

My mom's not perfect, but she's always been there for me and has taught me how to be strong.

What gives our kids security and strength? Mom, it's not your perfection! It's your presence that makes kids feel secure. Drop the television image and just be the woman you are. Your courageous feats will most likely lead to one of two results:

either failure or success. And neither result is quite what you might expect. For instance, your failure may be very freeing for kids. (We'll discuss that further in a later chapter.) Real failure is failing to finish a race because you think you must be an unequivocal success.

A mom preoccupied with success may serve to separate her child from a secure feeling that she is real, close, and present. Susan's mom is near the top, but she doesn't expect her mom to be tops. Remember, *presence*, not *perfection*, blesses your child with security.

Fourteen-year-old Jeremy says:

I'm thankful for her always being there for me and I love her.

If he were to paint his mom with a color, Jeremy would select green. He says:

My mom brings life wherever she goes. She is always happy and positive.

Jeremy is secure and full of life when his mom is present. At fourteen, in the critical years of early adolescence, Jeremy needs a great deal of security so he can blast off into his teenage world. His mom's positive, happy nature gives him the green-light to go and grow.

Linnsey Workman, a teenage journalist from Mission Viejo, California wrote an article in her local paper describing the last few weeks before high school graduation. She portrays the battle of the expectations (modern day Battle of the Bulge) in a house with a teen. She writes: "We expect not to have curfews, yet we still want Mommy to make our beds in the morning."[2]

The issue is not who makes the bed. Linnsey helps us realize kids still value the security of knowing mom will be there to help shore up life. Security means peace. A local art gallery was having a contest to find what artist could best depict that word. The gallery walls were filled with entries of peaceful meadows full of beautiful flowers, majestic mountains covered with snow, and calm waters with a single sailboat floating on still water. In the midst of all of these beautiful, powerful scenes portraying peace, the judges selected one particular artwork as the winner: a painting of a large tree blowing in the wind. The sky was dark and filled with horrific storm clouds. Leaves were swirling around the ground. In the fork of the tree between two branches sat a mother bird with a few small chicks under her wings. The winning painting was entitled, "Peace."

Mom, your presence does not keep storms at bay, but it does provide security and peace in the midst of the storms. Fifteen-year-old Jessica paints her portrait of mom with the color yellow:

My mom can be compared to the sun because she is always watching over me.

Moms who are always there bless their children with security. Mom's presence also provides a second blessing—acceptance.

2. The Blessing of Acceptance

Security says, "I'm here." Acceptance says, "I am here for you, and I will be here for you when you return." Fifteen-year-old Brandi says it well:

Thanks for being there when I needed you.

What does it take to truly accept your child?

Acceptance means responding with your heart, not your head.

Acceptance means valuing the child over the child's action.

Acceptance takes the long-term perspective of potential and change, not the immediate perspective of pain and conflict.

Acceptance means approaching a child with care not judgment, compassion not criticism.

Acceptance means ranking "who" over "what" and "why."

Fifteen-year-old Van has a mother who knows what it means to accept her child:

Mom, thanks for always being there for me, and thanks for understanding.

Mom, when you are there, you show you understand. The child says, "Not just one time, but time after time you were there for me."

Earlier we introduced you to a young person named Hannah. Allow us to tell you a little more about her and her mom. She rated her relationship with her mom a nine on a scale of one to ten. A high rating for Hannah's mother! What's behind her mom's success? Hannah tells us:

Everybody has their ons and offs and we are pretty close. We can talk to each other about anything. Our relationship is always there for me to lean on.

Even though Hannah's relationship is like a switch going on and off (remember, presence—not perfection—counts), they remain close.

A song entitled "Lean on Me" had its first run decades ago, but a remake with a contemporary feel brought the tune back to kids of the 90s. (It's one of the few songs today both parents and child can listen to and find a mutually satisfying message!) The song has one clear message: "Lean on me, when you're not strong and I'll be your friend, I'll help you carry on."

No doubt Hannah would think the song was written by her mother. Being there provides an acceptance that communicates, "I understand and I will be here for you to lean on." Mom's presence blesses the child. And Mom's presence is a source of encouragement.

3. The Blessing of Encouragement

Fifteen-year-old Ciara describes her mom as the color yellow: warm and bright. She's just the best mom in Ciara's eyes. How does her relationship with her mom rate? Stand up and cheer with Ciara. Their relationship is an eight. Why?

My mom and I are very close; we share our problems with each other. When one of us is down we cheer the other up.

Ciara and her mom have built a relationship upon layers and layers of blessings. Ciara is blessed with security because she and her mom are close. She is blessed because she has found acceptance. And she is blessed because she and her mom encourage each other. How important are these blessings of security, acceptance, and encouragement to Ciara? She told us in her definition of a mother.

Mom, do you want a good three-point job description for

your role as a mother? Learn from Ciara what it takes to do the job. After she said

My mom and I are very close. We share our problems with each other. When someone is down we cheer the other up.

she added, *That's how all mothers should be.*

Mom, what is your job?

1. Stay close.
2. Share conflicts.
3. Send cheers.

4. The Blessing of Tenacity

Do you have a friend who has been through divorce and is trying to find the tenacity—-the stick-to-it-iveness—to stuff all her belongings in a suitcase, make life changes after the divorce, and keep on walking? Fifteen-year-old Tracey told us about her mom. She said:

I love you so much. You have been there through thick and thin. When we had nothing but a suitcase, you kept on walking to win the victory. You gave us a beautiful home, and our lives are back together. Thank you and thank God!

What happens when moms hang in there and press on toward the goal? Their kids are showered with the blessing of tenacity, making it through thick and thin in their own lives. Some of us know this blessing firsthand.

When Doug thinks of "thick and thin," a few images come to mind: Crown Point Elementary School, *TV Guide* deliveries by bike, *The Courtship of Eddie's Father,* bowling, Marquis Manor Apartments, Lakers games on the radio. These images probably mean nothing to you, but to Doug they are benchmarks in his childhood.

"After my parents' divorce I learned firsthand what it meant to be tenacious without ever knowing the word existed. Even though my parents were apart, they taught me one of my greatest assets: the ability to hang in there through thick and thin.

"My folks divorced when I was eight years old. We three boys started living with Mom. Then our parents decided it was best for boys to be raised by their dad. It was an unusual arrangement back then and still uncommon today. In my research for writing *Dear Dad,* I discovered less than 2 percent of children from divorced homes in the 70s grew up with their dads. We Websters were rare indeed.

"After some time with dad and my brothers, I needed my mom. So I packed my one suitcase and headed south for San Diego. I moved into Mom's two-bedroom apartment, and we set out together to live a new life. I enrolled in a school called Crown Point Elementary. I still remember the day my classmate brought a snake sandwich to school. (All I had was good ole peanut butter and jelly. Although my sandwich brought less interest, it still had more bargaining power. Who wants to trade an apple for a rattlesnake on Wonder Bread covered with Kraft single-slice American cheese and Miracle Whip?)

"The old classroom building with the wall of counter-to-ceiling, crank-out windows felt like a military training center.

I remember my after-school delivery route of *TV Guide* magazine. I think it paid eleven cents per guide! If I finished my route in time, I could enjoy one of my favorite TV shows, *The Courtship of Eddie's Father*. Eddie became a mentor for me. 'Keep on going, Doug. You and your mom can make it because my Dad and I are figuring that out successfully.'

"My mom reminds me of the time I encouraged her to go out bowling one night when she really did not feel like being social. 'Leave me with a baby-sitter if need be and go to the Halloween bowling party,' I said. Somehow I knew Eddie would have said the same thing to his father.

"Today she is grateful for the encouragement from her nine-year-old son. That night she met a man she later married and to whom she is still married, nearly twenty-five years later. Tenacity means doing things you really don't feel like doing. My mom was a single mom with a new job in a foreign community without much support. I admired her courage.

"The short season changed for me, and I was compelled to return to live with my dad and my two brothers—my fourth move in less than two years. The four male Websters moved from our home alongside the tenth fairway of a country club golf course to the alley side of the Marquis Manor Apartments. My father was an engineer when it seemed like every other kid's dad in southern California had the same job. Soon defense contractors no longer needed as many engineers; he was laid off along with thousands of others.

"The two-bedroom place in Marquis Manor Apartments, not much larger than the place where I'd lived with my mom, had to house four of us. My older brothers took the room on the side near the carport. My dad took the front room. My options were limited. At age eleven, I became my dad's roommate.

"As unusual as the living arrangement was, it was great for a young man who wanted to connect with his dad. I can still recall the nights we lay in the dark listening to L.A. Laker basketball games on the radio. The game would finish and my heroes—Jerry West, Wilt Chamberlain, or Elgin Baylor— would be interviewed in the post-game. Chick Hearn offered his final commentary on the game, and then he would say, 'On behalf of the the entire Laker organization, thank you and good night.' Then Dad would turn the radio off and say, 'Good night, son. Now, get some sleep.'

"I don't think Eddie ever had to share a room with his father. How lucky for his dad! How unfortunate for Eddie. Every day I saw my dad rise, shave, get dressed, and head out to find a new job to secure a better life for his three boys and himself, often with nothing more than tenacity in his hand."

Earlier you read Nick's comment:"

We are always there for each other and we have both been through a lot together.

Mom, being there doesn't mean perfection. It means being present. Unfortunately sometimes that presence is interrupted. What happens when mom is separated from her child? Erika, at age fifteen, offers hope to moms in this situation. She says:

I love you Mom, very much. Even though eight hours and about

4,000 miles come between us, you are always in my heart and in my thoughts.

You can still bless your child with the gift of tenacity. And sometimes you will experience "a blessing boomerang." Your child returns the blessing to you. Do you ever need someone to help you hang in there during your labor of love? We'll let Kellie, age fourteen, explain:

Mom, I love you dearly. I realize I hurt your feelings a lot, but I never mean to. Through it all, I know you'll be there for me, just like I hope you know I'll be there for you, always and forever.

Tenacious moms teach kids how to hang in there. Tenacious kids learn how to be there for mom when she needs them.

The blessing of security, the blessing of acceptance, the blessing of encouragement, and the blessing of tenacity are a result of mom being there for her child.

WHAT'S A MOTHER TO DO?

Motherhood is an enormous labor of love that shifts dramatically at about age thirteen, then drops drastically in raw time around age sixteen to a final few years, which are very high in intensity.

What can a mother do to enhance the time she spends with her child as the person grows from the cradle to the commencement service? Here are four practical ways to make the most of your being there with your child.

1. Date Your Child

In the beginning of Chapter 1, we introduced you to a young eleven-year-old friend named Jennifer. She was the one who said:

My mom is the best mom in the whole universe. I love her sooooo much.

(Her emphasis, not ours!)

How does this universally spectacular mom rate? This young gal says a ten. Jennifer explains why:

We like to spend time together. We've attended Mother /Daughter Conferences for five years.

Mom's secret is time spent with her daughter. Almost all eleven-year-olds like to be with mom. More importantly, Jennifer perceives that mom likes to spend time with her daughter. Ever since Jennifer was six, her mom would pack their camp clothes, say good-bye to home and all it entailed, and take off for the annual Mother/Daughter conference. Nothing but the mountains, the fresh air, and time with mom!

Mom, any resources in your life that can help you bless your child with time together? What if you can't afford to go to camp? Listen to what our friend Tracey, age fifteen, has to say:

My mom is my best friend. We go to dinners, movies, concerts. I can come to her with any problem, and she will guide me through the trial. I love her with all my heart.

It doesn't seem to matter to Tracey what she and her mom do or where they go. Mom, unless you are with your child, you will not find the chance for your child to love you with all of his or her heart.

You can count on the powerful blessings your child receives when he or she looks to you and says, *Mom, you're always there.* Here are some practical ways to maximize your time with your child.

Once we started dating our three kids one-on-one, they could not get enough of the experience. Will your kids like the idea? Listen to the advice one young person gave another young person who had a workaholic mom:

> *Ask your mom to set aside a certain day of the week (or month) to spend with you. Let her know how much you want to be with her and suggest you keep the day (or evening) for each other.*
> Julie from Mississippi[3]

If Julie recommends it, maybe your child will accept the prescription. Most kids we know do. They value being with you, Mom.

What happens if moms neglect time with their kids? Potential relationships with a "10" rating quickly drop down the scale. Listen to what some young people told us:

> *Stop and spend some time with me. My relationship with my mom is a three because she spends more time with my sisters.*
> Jon, twelve years old

Kimberly, age thirteen, struggles with the same issue as Jon. She says:

Our relationship is a five. It is not an open relationship because we don't spend time together.

That's probably how younger kids feel, especially young girls, you say. Wrong. Read on:

I want to spend more time together. Our relationship is a seven because
we really don't do much together, but when we do, we get along.
Steve, sixteen years old

Is he alone? No. A peer his same age with the same name told us his relationship with mom was an eight because . . .

We don't spend tons of time together.

Before we move on to practical suggestion number two, let us offer a caution to this idea of dating your child. We don't propose it as a substitution for dating your spouse, or if you are a single mom, for dating a friend. Kids are not ready to become mom's dates. The dating we recommend with you and your child is not intended to fulfill any of the relational benefits of adult dating. Date your spouse first; then date your kids. This is the order that started the family in the first place.

2. Write a Love Letter

One of the simplest, most powerful ways to bless your child is to write him or her a love letter. Take some time today to jot a note to your child, telling how much he or she means to you. To go the next step, stop by a card store or make a personalized card at home for your child. Best step yet is to mail the card to your child. Who of us doesn't love to get a card in the mail from someone who expresses love and appreciation?

You might write on the card ten to twenty qualities you admire in your child. Remember, don't look for perfection, look for the presence of these qualities, however minuscule they may be. When you highlight them, we guarantee they will blossom.

One of the hopes of Dear Mom is to prompt young people to share the thoughts they shared with us with their moms. Imagine the mom who gets a card from a child communicating:

Mom, you are the color gold because you shine inside and out.
Love, Emilie

Mom, you are the color yellow because you have tons of energy and you flow with the radiance of love.
Love, Emily

Mom, our relationship would be a 10, but we have our moments. So I give us a 9.8. I love you.
Love, Emily

These different girls with the same name are sending the same love to three different moms. Imagine how those moms feel! The great benefit of a love letter is you can read it again and again. Mom, put down the book and pick up a pen. Send a love letter to your child.

3. Develop Time Management

Few moms we know are bored with little or nothing to do. Some think stay-at-home moms, like Robin, spend their days watching Oprah and eating bon-bons.

Moms work 24-hour shifts, lack vacation time, don't get regular breaks, and never get promotions or pay raises. And a growing number of moms work outside of the home besides, so you've got a lot of exhausted women looking for one thing: sleep. One young gal told us about her working mom's busy schedule. She said:

My relationship with my mom is a five. She works and is hardly ever home. It's hard to have a relationship with a mom who is not around.
Misty, fourteen years old

What can moms, especially working moms, do to maximize their time with their children? Here's an idea. Do what we did: Ask the children. Involve your children in the decision making to help you prioritize your time and to educate them on the awesome role of being a mom. Without beating them with a guilt stick ("You know I'm doing this just for you"), let your child know why you do what you do with your time.

Honest communication brings understanding and leads to change.

According to Kay Willis, founder of Mothers Matter, one way working mothers can avoid resentment is to ask their employers to allow them to get home by 5:30 P.M. at least twice a week to play and eat with their young children.

In *Dear Dad* Doug addresses the demands of men who are trying to combine career with fatherhood.[3] As a mom, you may find some value from his practical suggestions for integrating time and money with family. More and more women are facing the struggle dads encounter to keep kids and work in balance.

We invite you to look at Appendix C for a way to make a lasting commitment to your child. In our culture of nonexistent rites of passage for our kids, you may find this refreshing and meaningful.

FIND A TREE IN THE STORM

Our final word for you, Mom, is to find a tree in the storm. The victorious painting, "Peace," portrayed a mother bird keeping her chicks safe from the storm. Her strength was not found in fighting the storm. Her success was secured when she found a strong set of arms in which to rest.

Mom, who do you turn to when you run out of places to hide? The labor of love called motherhood demands more than any one woman can supply on her own. Who is helping you raise your kids? Are you strong enough to meet your family's expectations? How would you respond if the following comment from a twenty-year-old who chose to remain anonymous was aimed at you?

I wish my mom was stronger at times, but because she is who she is, I am who I am.

Do you expect to be a Hollywood-designed supermom?

At first glance, some of the kids we heard from might as well have had Devon Adair or Captain Janeway as their moms. Tracey says her mom is the color white because:

White is the color to show love, patience, caring. She's beautiful.

Could it be we found a real live television heroine? Not so. Look closer.

She has been through many trials, but God is in her heart. He's glorified through it.

Much like Lee Iacocca's mom during the Depression, Tracey's mom had someone to cling to in the midst of the storm. Her mom received safety and God got the glory. She did not do it as a solo flight—mother against the elements.

The psalmist states:

"The Lord is my rock and my fortress and my deliverer; My God, my strength, in whom I will trust."[4]

Mom, don't stand alone. Place yourself in the strong arms of love to keep your family safe. It may mean setting Dear Mom down and offering a prayer from the heart. Or you may need to find a friend with whom you can share your feelings of the pending or surrounding storm. You may want to call and ask if you can meet with a minister. Mom, your child will never be able to hear you sing "Lean on Me" if you can't stand. Don't settle for a TV image. Be yourself and find the "Tree of Life" in which you will be safe.

When children can truly say, Mom, you are always there, they will find themselves with a handful of blessings: security, acceptance, encouragement, and tenacity. The relationship is likely to release the boomerang blessing and shower mom in return.

In her address to the graduating class at Wellesley College, Barbara Bush offered these thoughts:

As important as your obligation as a doctor, a lawyer, or a business leader may be, your human connections with your spouse, your children, and your friends are the most important investment you will ever make. At the end of your life, you will never regret not having passed one more test, not winning one more verdict, or not closing one more deal, but you will regret time not spent with your spouse, your children, or your friends.[5]

We finish the chapter as we began, with words from kids who had moms who implement the wisdom the former First Lady passed on.

My mom is the color yellow. She can be compared to the sun because she is always watching over me.
Jessica, fifteen years old

My mom is like the sun shining bright twenty-four hours a day.
Kristin, fourteen years old

Dear Mom,

Thank you for always being there for me and for spending time with me. I feel secure knowing you are here to understand, encourage, and support me. You are like the sun bringing life and warmth to me.

Love,
Your child

CHAPTER 3

> *Dear Mom,*
>
> *You're always there!*
>
> *Love,*
> *Your child*

MOM, YOU'RE ALWAYS THERE!

Sometimes she's not always going to agree with the decisions I make, but she can't live my life. I need to make my own decisions and learn by them.

Jennifer, seventeen years old

Mom, get off your nagging horse. When you're not nagging, you're great! You need to trust me more. I'm a good girl.

Kendra, sixteen years old

We possess an open relationship, but I often become angry at her for being over-protective.

Josh, fifteen years old

Comedian Robin Williams once said, "If it's not one thing, it's your mother." Mom, are you trying too hard?

What happens when you get a plurality of moms, too many or too much of one? You add an *s* to the word *mother*. No, not *mothers*. That's a cookie brand. Put the *s* at the other end. Too much mother or too many mothers equals *smother*.

The first message of the four negative messages—Cries of the Heart—is *Mom, you're* always *there!*

The endearing words in the last chapter are coming through again, minus the positive spin. The tone says everything. As you read the phrase, *Mom, you're* always *there,* this time say it out loud. When you get to the word always, clench your teeth as you speak. When you reach the word *there,* draw it out. Right away you will pick up what young people mean by this second message to moms.

Mom, you're always *theeeerrrrrreee!*

One young gal helped us understand what her peers mean when she filled out our survey. She gave her mom a ten on the rating scale. Why? She writes:

My mom is watching me fill this out.

The kid could not even get a few private minutes to let us know what she thought about her mom! Her mom's effort to make sure she looked good was the very thing that soured her for her daughter. Too much mom equals smother. Fourteen-year-old Chae's one request to mom is:

Give me a little privacy.

Remember the warm comments made by a few kids in the last chapter, likening their moms to the sun? Another young girl also compared her mom to the sun by labeling her the color red. Why?

My mom has red hair, freckles, and is always sunburned.

Like the sun on her mom's skin, what happens when you get too much of a good thing. You get burned. This young girl goes on to say her relationship with her mom is a three. Why?

We don't get along too well. I love her, but we're too much alike.

To this thirteen-year-old, her mom is a mirror. Anyone, regardless how narcissistic, will grow tired of peering into a mirror at one's own reflection. Mom, when you stand too close, too long, or act too much like your child, someone is going to get burned—or run to get as far away from the heat as possible. Some kids need momburn lotion with a high SPF rating.

One of our favorite children's stories is "The Runaway Bunny." One day a bunny tells his mother that he wants to run away by turning into someone or something different. Yet when the bunny wants to become a fish, the mother says she'll become a fisherman and catch the bunny. When the bunny declares he will become a sailboat, the mother says she will become the wind and blow the boat back to the mother's harbor. One bunny fantasy after another is matched by the mother rabbit's transformation. Eventually the bunny concludes he might as well stick around home with mom.

Granted, it is a precious story, especially for moms. But, what if the bunny is in his mid-teen years, desperately trying to leave the burrow to become a hare. Will he make it? Not with mom being one step ahead of him. The story takes on a whole new meaning if you look at it this way. Is it the goal of a mother rabbit to set the bunny free? Might the bunny feel the same way as Robin Williams if this maternal trap continues? That's a lucky rabbit's foot we do not want to hang on anyone.

Mom, don't get us wrong. We are not proponents of running away from home. We live in a dangerous world that is far from make-believe stories and children's fables. But if you keep the little hare in the hole the whole time, he'll never learn life's valuable lessons from the likes of the tortoise or Mr. McGregor.

Allows us to dial in a few of these internal, potentially eternal messages on the mom/child network.

MOM, IF I COULD TELL YOU ANYTHING . . .

Twelve-year-old Juli informed us of her strong relationship with her mom. *It's a nine,* she said. What knocks it down a notch?

Sometimes she takes control of what I'm doing.

As we poured through those responses from hundreds of young people, many of them let us know mom is the boss of their life. Not all of them are crazy about this arrangement. Listen to the emotion behind these kids if they could say anything to mom:

Too strict. Need more independence.
Jennie, thirteen years old

Let me lead my own life. Give me space and more responsibility. Life is difficult to understand. Stop trying to treat me like a kid.
Kelly, twelve years old

Stop nagging and picking on my clothes.
Vanessa, thirteen years old

Leave me the %$#@%$#@ alone. Get out of my life!
Tim, thirteen years old

We will talk about anger in Chapter 7. For now let us focus

on the cause of a significant amount of childhood frustration: mom's control.

Notice, Mom, these kids are very bold in their declarations of independence. Secondly, these kids want to do more on their own. They want more self-control. Thirdly, they are predominantly young teenagers. The stage of early adolescence gives parenting a bad name. In this stage kids are bucking the system that seemed to be working so nicely in the late grade school years. Back then, they understood the rules. They were self-sufficient in the areas of personal hygiene and maintenance. They still retained some semblance of respect for mom and/or dad's power. They were physically small and hormonally stable to keep the physiological monsters corralled for the current time being. Then one day a teenager gets out of bed and mom mutters, "I feel as though I have awakened a sleeping giant!"

THE POWER BATTLE

Bottom-line question for a growing young person is: Who is in control? How would you answer the question for your family? Use the following tool to rate your answers:

The Power Bar

MOM————————————————CHILD

Consider these questions:
1. Where do you put a mark to determine the control? 50/50? 80/20? 30/70?

2. Has the benchmark moved right (towards the child) in the past few years?

3. Where would your child place the mark?

Young people want to know: will there be a shift in the family's balance of power anytime soon?

When the Power Is Left with Mom

In many families, mom is in total control. As a result, kids learn control is king. So they conclude, I need to be in control when mom is not around.

What if they can't gain control of a situation they find themselves in? They say to themselves, Since I'm not in control, I'll act childish. They de-mature, so to speak. If they can't control, they end up giving away control that belongs to them. They blame, shame, neglect, deny, whatever it takes to say, *Look, you're the boss. It's not my job.* Now Mom, suppose your child is facing a decision on an athletic team or in a class group project—or just a casual choice, such as picking a movie to watch or where to go for dinner. He or she quickly realizes, *I don't know how to share control.* The child either grabs power and loses friends or abandons involvement and alienates his pals. He or she will take this pattern into adult decisions that affect marriage, family, and occupation.

Mommie dearest, this is the strongest negative message we heard! Kids are serious. When a mommie dearest over-protects, she controls. When she controls, she smothers. When she smothers, she chokes. When she chokes, the child dies—sometimes a slow and painful death.

We've mentioned what kids do when mom over-controls. Now travel with us as we unveil the internal messages kids learn when mom says, "I'm the boss."

What Kids Learn from a Maternal Mandate

Powerful messages enter the mind of a young person when he or she is bound by a mommie dearest. Mom, do you want your child to hear you saying:

- "You are incapable."
  The child responds by thinking: "I really can't do it at all. If I could, Mom would let me. I'm no good at this."
- "You are dependent."
  And the child responds: "Since I can't do it, Mom has to do it. She always has and she always will. I can't do it without Mom around."
- "You better not fail."
  The child then responds, "It must be so important that Mom has to do it for me or make sure I do it under adult supervision. So if I mess up or fail, I'm in trouble. I can't fail."
- "You cannot conquer the fear."
  And the child responds, "It must be quite scary otherwise Mom would let me do it without her. The fear is bigger than I thought. I better not try to do it on my own."

- "You are not worth trusting."

  The child thinks: "My mom does not trust me. I must not be trustworthy. Plus, trust is a risky thing. So, I'll avoid trusting anyone."

We parents do not want our children (or spouses) to receive these messages, but believe us, they do.

Is there hope? The kids we talk with sure think so. Listen to young person, Saran, age fourteen.

My mom is the color white. She is always open to new ideas. She can easily change her ways if necessary.

How can a mother remedy the situation and become more like Saran's mom who brings some bright color to the family?

WHAT'S A MOTHER TO DO?

1. Use Your Brain.

Mom, you have a brain. You also have the brawn as an authoritative parent. Don't give up either asset. But don't overuse the brawn of power because the brain is disengaged. The kids we hear from in this chapter have moms who use more wrestling than reasoning. Sit down and define the goals you want to accomplish. Avoid decisions based on emotion. How do we employ the head over the heart? Work. Nothing short of clear thinking and hard work will put your brain in gear.

2. Define Your Purpose.

What are you trying to accomplish as a mother of your child? In the Webster family, we're trying to teach self-government. We want to raise responsible kids. If they can control themselves, they are more able to choose the appropriate responses: they will be response-able. Then we know Brookelyn, Jamie, and Chase will limit or be able to manage the conflict that comes their way. They will be equipped to make a difference in the lives of those around them. And as they grow up, they will be less dependent on mom and dad so we can spend more time together. Remember, it was our love for each other that got us into this predicament in the first place. We are just working diligently to get back to the starting point, with the exception of a mere twenty-five-year diversion to raise a few kids. We're not about to let five Webster family members spin out of control and ruin a great thing that began for us in the early '80s. Each of our three children are plodded, encouraged, corralled, and disciplined toward self-control—not other-control.

Mom, every time you make a decision involving your child, ask yourself, "How will it help my child grow to be one step closer to self-control?" The child will never reach the goal if the mother and father have not taken the disciplined steps to figure out the parents' role first. Here is a way to help you define your target as a parent. Finish this statement:

"When my child reaches age eighteen, I hope he/she will _____."

Use qualities or characteristics obtainable by a young adult. Begin where you are now and establish the tracks to help your child reach this target. If the child is older, invite the child's participation. Remember, self-government is the goal, otherwise you will raise a generation of dependent children anticipating entitlements at every turn. Once you establish the target, discover your role in the partnership.

3. Define Your Job.

In Chapter 2 we took the words of one of our young advisors and created a simple three-part job description for mothers. According to Ciara, here's what a mother should do:

1. Stay close.
2. Share conflicts.
3. Send cheers.

Ciara is not a family management consultant or a parenting expert, but she is the beneficiary of what she calls a very effective mom.

What other major responsibilities would you add to Ciara's starter job description for moms? Take a few minutes to write out five to ten top responsibilities of your job as a mom. Next, go back to each one and apply a measurable goal. For example, you may put *cook* as a vital task in your job. The goal could be, "As the family cook, I will do the planning, shopping, and cooking to offer seven healthy dinners each week." Mom, take note of a few things:

- *Seven* dinners a week. That means one meal per night, not two to three meals per night, depending upon each child's preference.
- Seven *dinners* a week. Let's assume your child is older. Mom, he can prepare his own breakfast and lunch. You buy the sandwich fixings, bread, and cereal, then point him to the refrigerator. Remember, self-government is the goal!
- *Planning.* Planning means no family member screams into the kitchen at 5:30 P.M. (we call this FST, Family Standard Time) to say, "Mom, can we have pizza instead of that stuff you're cookin'?"

Mom, you're heading for defeat if you don't use your brain. Consider this scenario: It's late, you're full steam ahead over a hot stove after a long day, and your kid is setting you up to either back down in retreat or advance and answer, "Because I'm the mom, I'm the cook, and I said *no!*" to his appeal for pizza. Your child will walk away thinking he wants to send a survey to the Websters telling them what an ogre of a mother he has. What if you responded, "Son, I appreciate your creativity. I go shopping at the beginning of each week. If you could remind me then, I'd be happy to procure all the goods we need for your meal. Right now I'm planning for a wonderful dinner of Hamburger Helper. I'd love to have you join us if you choose. Otherwise, you know how to fix your breakfast in the morning and I bet you'll be hungry." Your son will walk away bewildered by your rational response, thinking to himself, *Mom's been reading too many motherhood books.*

4. Define What Kids Need.

Kids need two vital elements to help them grow up in a world that is falling apart: morals and models. And they are looking to you, parents, to supply these items.

Morals are the boundaries and behaviors you expect from your child. They refer to critical issues such as church involvement, drinking, drugs, money, sex, school attendance, and grades. We live in a culture where young people desperately need guard rails to keep them from pending disaster. In *Drug Proof Your Kids,* Jim Burns and Stephen Arterburn write: "Kids today are making decisions about alcohol and drugs when they are twelve to fourteen years old, whereas in the preceding generation they made those decisions at ages sixteen to eighteen."[1]

Morals establish off-limit zones and boundaries for your child. (Valuable tools for parents on these topics are available in Appendix B.) One example of a boundary is allowing your child to attend a party supervised by parents. Another example: Expect your child's complete abstention from any alcohol use. Let's face it, few kids want rules. Rules inconvenience them, but they also provide guard rails to keep them safe along the roads they travel. Even kids can see the value in the boundaries. A young girl named Amanda told us,

Mom, you bug me with rules, but they're helpful.

Kids need and want morals. They also look for models of how to live.

Models are obviously adults who live out the values they expect children to honor. Mom, is it time to check your own boundaries and behaviors? True, adults are given freedoms that children must earn. Help your child understand this truth. A child cannot legally drive a car until age sixteen, regardless of the frequency, volume, or intensity of his tantrums. He can't "out pout" the law. Many control conflicts arise in families where parents say, "Do as I say, not as I do." One thirteen-year-old told us:

Mom, practice what you preach!

Kids won't integrate your values if you don't value integrity. What do you see when you look in the mirror? Will Maria remain sexually pure in a home where her mom is promiscuous? Chances are high the daughter will be sexually active by her mid-teen years, likely sooner. Another personal question of challenge: What do you see when you look behind the mirror? What kind of prescription pills placate the pain in your present and past? Will Johnny avoid the temptation of a beer buzz at a bash when mom's body is the victim of her Valium vice? Not likely.

On the other hand, kids model most closely those who stay close to them. Listen to the influence Olivia's mom has on her daughter's life:

My mom is a trusted friend to me. We respect one another.

Respect is based on compassion and character, not control and conflict. We believe if we walked into Olivia's home and met her mom, we would be treated with respect. Kids don't want magazine-cover moms. Being a model means more than a cover girl looking good; it means living for the good of the child. And our children are watching our every step.

You've defined your purpose, your job, and your child's needs. Once those are up and working, it is time to put the young brain to work.

5. Use Your Child's Brain

Mom, we present you with a few case studies to let you practice using your brain and the brain your child came equipped with at birth. Then we follow with some thoughts we've picked up over the years for working the cobwebs out of our brains.

Parents' G.P.A. It's Sunday night at 8:55 P.M. Your fifth grader is ready to brush his teeth and head for sleepland. As he climbs into bed, he suddenly gasps and says, "Mom, I forgot about my science project. It's due tomorrow. I'm supposed to have a poster board with pictures of fifteen different types of mammals, including their full species names. Can you help?"

Option 1: Mom throws on her favorite sweats and sneakers and drives down to the store at 9:37 P.M., Sunday evening, mumbling to herself the whole way. She roams the school supplies aisle, looking for poster board and glue. She stops briefly to say hello to three other moms from her son's class. Together they ransack the store. Desperately trying to remember the difference between a reptile, a mammal, and a bird, mom scans the magazine section and selects a copy of *Dogs Today,* then heads home for her late night, cut-and-glue session.

Option 2: Mom says, "Son, I'm sorry you waited until tonight to recall your homework. You know we have a rule that says all homework is to be finished by dinner on Sunday night. If you wake up early, I am willing to take you down to the store in the morning to help you get what you need. What would you like to do: get up early or go to class without your project? You decide.

(Son's mammal brain begins to function.)

Burger Bash. It's Friday afternoon around 1 P.M. Your four-year-old is going nutso, jumping up and down on the plastic balls in that lovely caged-in area, the play apparatus at the local fast-food BurgerLand. You've already told her, "Sweetie, I asked you to sit down and finish your meal. Mommy has to run a few errands before we pick up your brother at school. If you get up one more time, you're done with your meal." You know your husband is strict about keeping food out of the new family van, especially oily French fries and sticky ketchup in the hands of a four-year-old!

Option 1: Mom says another time or two, "Sweetie, I told you to sit down and eat," which is followed moments later by, "Okay, just for a few minutes, but don't expect me to buy you dessert before we leave BurgerLand." Seventeen minutes later, mom realizes the precious time she allotted for her errands is now tossed out like a multi-colored toy ball. She will have to

MOM, YOU'RE *ALWAYS* THERE! **55**

alter her plans for tomorrow to include a few extra errands. She is also left wearing something other than the perfect blouse tonight at the company dinner because it is held ransom at the cleaners.

After more time passes, little miss is up to her eyeballs in plastic balls, so mom shifts to the commando mode. "Alright, I've had it with you, young lady. Get out of there right now! We're leaving, and you just might never see this place again." BurgerLand comes to a halt as everyone stares at mom-gone-mad.

(Play is resumed only to repeat the scene minutes later with another family.)

Option 2: Mom says, "Sweetie, remember I said you had five minutes to finish lunch and no more getting up from the table? You're down to three minutes. Mommy is walking out the door with you in a little bit. I'm sure you expect to bring your food with you, but as you know, we have a rule about food in the new van. Here are your choices: Eat as much as you can in the next three minutes or get down now, and we'll leave early without the food. You can look forward to a great dinner tonight. What would you like to choose?"

(Daughter's mental apparatus begins to swing into action.)

Big Dance Basket Case. It's Wednesday evening around dinner time. Your eighth-grade daughter can't stop talking about the big dance coming up Friday night. It's her first dance and she is dying to go. She even gave her brand-new dress a test run at church on Sunday morning, only to receive rave reviews. One problem: On Sunday afternoon she dumped the dress in the laundry basket and left it there. It's piled under her brother's baseball pants and dad's garage grubbies.

You both have an agreement: As a fourteen-year-old young woman, she is in charge of the care and cleaning of her own clothes, including the items requiring professional dry cleaning. You're doing your best to let her control her destiny. You even prodded her the day before, knowing good and well that her dress was buried in a textile wasteland: "Honey, are you all ready for the dance? Got your dress, shoes, and stuff prepared?" "Yep, no problem, Mom. I am on top of things." Your subtle shove did not unveil her dirty dress dilemma.

It is Wednesday night and she has only one day left to attempt a twenty-four-hour dry cleaning or wear last year's Easter dress to this year's dance.

Option 1: Mom can't stand it any longer. The thought of her daughter not looking her best at her first dance is too much. Right after she takes the kids to school the next morning, she swings by the house, digs through the laundry basket, fishes out her daughter's prize possession, puts on her dark glasses, and heads straight for Speedy-Clean, which, by the way, is the only twenty-four-hour dry cleaner, and of course, is located across town. The rush order costs double. She picks up the dress Friday morning, removes the plastic from the hanger, and places the dress in her daughter's closet right above her glass slippers. As she walks out of the room, she mumbles to herself, "I know she'll appreciate looking her best. Plus, she will have plenty of future opportunities to develop responsibility."

Option 2: Come Friday afternoon, daughter has ransacked the house in search of her new dress with a vengeance equal to the FBI's pursuit of America's Most Wanted. Mom awaits an emotional explosion. The young girl blames her brother, her dad, the mailman, and the dog for the abduction of her dress. "Somebody is trying to sabotage my life and my first dance," she cries.

Mom tenderly walks up to her and says, "Honey, have you checked the laundry basket?" She gives mom that "No way, Mom, you must be an idiot" look. Then the color leaves her face as she remembers mom's earlier reminder. The house is momentarily silent until a burst comes from the hallway. "*Nooooooo!*" Mom is swift in consolation and then gently asks, "What would you like to do about the dance tonight? Do you want to stay home and miss out? Or do you have any other dresses that will work for the event? I'm here to help you get ready, sweetie."

(The girl's brain hits the dance floor and starts to spin!)

Mom, you may reach a different conclusion than we propose, but the more your child participates, the less you need to control. The less you control, the less you choke and the closer your child is to you.

We think moms ought to search out a knife, a life, and a lifeline.

MOMS NEED A KNIFE, A LIFE, AND A LIFELINE

Moms need a knife to cut the strings that tie them to their child. The umbilical cord was severed years ago. Are you still trying to be the sole source of support, guidance, control, and protection for your child? Mom, hear what the kids are saying. If you don't cut the apron strings, your child will sever the ties. And beware, Mom. It may take major surgery to reconnect with an offspring who has distanced him or herself far away from you. One fifteen-year-old girl told us to tell moms:

I know it's scary when kids are growing up, but you have to let us go.

Grab a knife and cut the cord, strand by strand if need be. Your child and you will be grateful in the long run.

Moms need a life too. Too many mothers are "married" to their kids. Mom, do you have a life that stands independent from your children? When asked, "How are you?" do you immediately start talking about the kids? If you don't have a life, is it because your child's life has become yours to live? There is only room for one life per person.

We're not talking family abandonment and maternal liberation. You made a choice years ago to be a mom, or you at least agreed to be involved in the activity that turns women into mothers. Being a mom is a labor of love but it was never designed to be a forfeiture of self. Sixteen-year-old Shaun gives his mom some very practical advice:

Mom, do something for yourself.

Moms also need a lifeline. Add to a mom's normal concerns the dangerous world in which we are raising kids today, and few parents want to send their child flying out of the nest. Letting go is easier (not easy, just easier) when you've got another person to lean on. That's why families most often work best when the child's mother and father are married to each other and committed to the child. You have the hand you need to help you let go of your child's hand.

We know what you're thinking, "But what if something goes wrong?" In other words, you're worried. And worry is a mom's inherent right, is it not? Fifteen-year-old Maddy told us:

Mom, don't worry even if it is your job.

Your child may leave forcefully and possibly prematurely, and that may lead to a child's destructive choices in an unsupervised life. Or your child may remain immature and forever dependent on mom. Is that what you want?

What keeps you from letting go? Is it the big bad world, your child's immaturity, or your need for control? Mom, grab a lifeline and give your child a new life.

A WORD TO MOMS ABOUT DADS

The movie *Honey, I Blew Up The Kids* has a classic line when the parents are called in to persuade their now 50-foot-tall baby to come with them. The dad says he will take care of the situation. His wife grabs his arm and says, "Honey, we all know daddies mean fun and mommies mean business."

All too true. Doug has an exhortation for you, Mom. Don't let dads get off so easy. Dad's not a deputy, he's a partner. Some moms are exhausted enforcers because their tendency to control the family keeps dad locked up in a cell with the convicted children. Set dad free to be involved in the parenting process.

We are always amazed at dads who say things like, "I never change poopy diapers," or "My wife is the one who gets up with the kids when they are sick." Too often dads do not know what to do. Mom, educate your guy. If you don't, you end up with two kids to raise, your child and him. He is competent. Remember, he was active in creating the child. If all else fails, give him the kid, the diaper bag, and say, "Honey, have a great time. I'll be back later." A good stench will prompt dad to fill the diaper pail quickly.

We suggest that you have dad help define your job, then do the same for him. If he does not know what to do, tell him to listen to the hundreds of kids who spoke up in Dear Dad. Encourage him to sit down and read the book, then compare notes with you. Ask each other which messages are different and which ones are similar. Work together, otherwise your kids will surround you, separate you, and leave your flank uncovered.

A WORD OF ENCOURAGEMENT TO HURTING MOMS

Life is an uncontrollable force circling us and our children. Job descriptions fall short to help a mother who comes from a background of pain and brokenness in her own relationship with her mom, her husband, or others. If you feel anchors of over-controlling or anger-laced action beneath the surface, call for help. Things will not get better because you read another book or try to use more brain power this time. Years of pain cannot be changed easily because you want to be a better mom. Your maternal aspirations are a powerful motivation, but not necessarily a catalyst for change. Call a friend, a pastor, a professional—someone who is there to help you leave a world of control.

Mom, we know part of your strong desire to "always be there" comes from the fear of what may happen when you can't be there. Life is an act of trust. Eventually you have to let the bunny out of the burrow. We trust in our children's ability to stay safe and live wise; we trust in other people to watch out for our loved ones; and we trust in a more powerful, more knowing God of love and protection. We are learning that the greatest investment of power is consistent prayer and less control. The best we can do is trust and hope.

Dear Mom,

You're always there—too much. Give me some space and privacy. Don't hold me too close or I'll push away and never come back. Let me go, let me grow. Just because I want to be more does not mean I think less of you.

*Love,
Your child*

CHAPTER 4

Dear Mom,

 I can tell
you anything.

Love,

Your child

I CAN TELL
YOU ANYTHING.

My relationship with my mom is a ten. My mom and I are very close.
I can talk to her about anything. I know she'll understand.

Megan, age fourteen

We are very close. I know that not all kids can talk to their mothers,
but I can.

Chris, age fifteen

My relationship with my mom is a ten. I can talk to her about
anything.

Chad, age fifteen
Holly, age nineteen
Jason, age seventeen
Josh, age fifteen
Melissa, age unknown
Richard, age thirteen
Tiffany, age thirteen

For nine years running, we Websters have journeyed to northern California in late August where Doug's dad and stepmom reside in beautiful Lake Wildwood. Our travel tradition began circa B.C. (Before Children). We now exist in the A.D. era (After Dominance by Children).

Every year we pack up our family vehicle and head off to

what we affectionately call "Camp Wildwood." The northern Websters live in a delightful home surrounded by majestic oaks and pines and nestled in the rolling hills of "49'er" country. The highlights of Camp Wildwood include George and Shirley's gracious and loving hospitality and Shirley's flair for gourmet cooking. We have a symbiotic relationship: Shirley loves to cook; we love to eat what she cooks.

Once filled with cuisinary delicacies, Doug and his dad always find time to get away for a father/son eighteen holes of golf. The beauty of the golf course setting overshadows the quality of the golf by far, but the father/son time is well worth the risk of public humiliation.

Now that the Webster offspring or "the blessed grandchildren" entered our lives (circa A.D.), the trip to grandpa and grandma's is a highlight of the year. The nearby private lake comes in handy to sprinkle the days with refreshing dips. Sometimes just getting away from one's own home offers the strength to make life worth facing again.

The down side of the glorious stay at grandpa and grandma's vacation getaway is the 520-mile gap between their home and ours. A few hundred of those miles are through the heart of California's central valley, abundant in agriculture but absent in aesthetics. Let's face it, a midday drive in 100-degree weather up Interstate 5 lacks appeal. (Our apologies to fellow Californians who call Coalinga home. The sight and aroma of the thousands of cattle just east of the highway is always a significant landmark for our trip.)

We are fortunate our kids travel well. Although we have

heard of some moms giving each child a dosage of the sleep-provoking, grape-flavored cold medicine called Dimetapp, "in case they get the sniffles," our kids travel an antihistamine-free highway. (Obviously we don't recommend drugs unless actual cold symptoms have been diagnosed.)

However, every now and then a Webster will get restless on the long haul, and we will resort to the radio to anesthetize our troupe. We are quick to run the gamut of Amy Grant and Raffi tapes. (Amy travels well. We recommend a sixty-mile rotation for Raffi to maintain parental sanity.) Then it is time to dial in the nearest radio station. Since our children are still pre-teen, we are yet to face the radio wars. (We do hear rumblings on the western flank from our oldest. More than finding a commonly desired music style, the challenge is to find any station on the van radio, preferably English-speaking. Country music is big on I-5, and since the family quickly tires of dad's crooning, the dial pops around frequently. Most often on those long road trips the radio station offers more static than music, more fuzz than fun.

Mom, life is like a family caravan trip. You pile in, hope you've got enough resources to make the long haul, select your destination or purpose for travel, and set out for the journey. Detours are inevitable. Rest stops are infrequent. Along the way, you find the common necessity to dial in.

This chapter is about tuning in. You and your family are somewhere along life's superhighway. You may be tired and feel far from home. If you are like the Webster family, every now and then the family gas tank runs dangerously close to empty.

When we asked a thousand young people about their moms, one of the strongest, most consistent messages we received was a child's ability or inability to "tune in" to mom. The second question on our survey was:

If I were to rate my relationship with my mom on a scale of one to ten (ten being the highest), mine would be a _____ because . . .

And here is what resulted from that question: Communication between mother and child determines the value of the relationship.

You would think the second question we asked the young people was, "How well do you and your mom communicate?" We didn't. Our question was more general, but the responses were geared toward how each child can or cannot talk with mom. More specifically, the dominant response from young people to the question of a relationship rating involved:

How well my mom knows me.

Some kids' communication with their moms could be compared to a favorite music station (which is quite a compliment coming from a young person). Some children might as well say there are times when the station is clear and other times when there is nothing but static. Some young people let us know they can find the mom-channel, but it comes across in a foreign language, hard to understand and meaningless after moments of listening. A few don't even care to know mom's radio call numbers and whether she is on the AM or FM frequency.

Mom, how well do you know your child? Are you dialed in to him or her? And can your child find you on his or her receiver? The answers to these questions are both in and out of your control. One way you can know more about your child is by watching the child closely—exercising your own intuition, which can be defined as "in-to-it." Many women exercise this "mother's intuition" very effectively. If you feel like you missed this gift, don't worry. Intuition can be nurtured. We call it being a student of your child. (And you can always call upon an astute friend to confirm your intuition.)

A second and more critical way to know more about your child is largely out of your control. Mom, you cannot control how much your child is willing to tell you. We hope you gave up the desire to control after reading the last chapter. You can try to pry it or pull it out like many moms do, but it won't work initially or if it does, it will backfire in the long run. Eventually your pressure will send relational steam into the air and cloud the relationship. Picture your interpersonal communication with your child as a teacher/student relationship. You, Mom, are *the student* and you will only learn from the teacher (your child) what he or she is willing to teach you. Learn the difference between control and influence. You cannot control: you can't force a professor to profess what they don't know or don't want you to know. You *can* influence: You can prepare yourself and the classroom or home to be as conducive to teaching as possible.

This chapter deals with the positive side of a mother's communication with her child, what we call Talk from the Heart. After reviewing hundreds of comments from kids, we found four levels of communication. The level in this chapter is: *Mom, I can tell you anything*.

Chapter 5 discusses the other levels of communication between a child and a mom:

Mom, I can tell you almost anything.
Mom, I can't tell you everything.
Mom, I can't tell you anything.

We discovered that kids go directly to *what mom knows about me* to qualify and quantify their relationship with mom. We took the group of young men and women who discussed communication with their moms, attached the rating of their relationship with their moms, and then placed them in the four levels of communication. We then established an average for each of the different levels. Here is a numerical look at the four types of communication messages:

The Child's Message	The 1 to 10 Scale Averages
Mom, I can tell you anything.	9.45
Mom, I can tell you almost anything.	8.26
Mom, I can't tell you everything.	8.0
Mom, I can't tell you anything.	5.14

Specifically, the more mom knows about the child (as broadcast by the child and received by mom), the stronger the relationship. We did find that three-and-a-half times as many girls as boys referred to communication, but as you will read later in the chapter, young men also placed high value on communicating with mom. The more your child feels like he or she can tell you and the more you know in the process, the higher your relationship climbs on your child's scale.

Let's clarify the four levels to better understand the meaning behind the child's message when he or she talks about a relationship with mom:

The Child's Message	The Child's Meaning
I can tell anything to my mom.	We have a great relationship.
I can tell almost anything to my mom.	We have a good relationship.
I can't tell everything to my mom.	We have an okay relationship.
I can't tell anything to my mom.	We have a lousy relationship.

Those messages and the meaning behind them say a great deal to you, Mom. If you are blessed, you may someday receive a comment like the ones we heard from many young people. Alexis and Christopher are two fifteen-year-olds, one female and one male, who let us know of a rare privilege they possess:

I CAN TELL YOU ANYTHING. 71

a close relationship with their moms secured by strong communication. Hear their words:

> *We have good communication compared to that of my friends'*
> *relationships with their moms.*
> Alexis, age fifteen

> *We are very close. I know that not all kids can talk to their mothers,*
> *but I can.*
> Christopher, age fifteen

These kids realize that not all moms and kids communicate well. Mom, if you can dial in to your child, congratulations. If you can't, don't give up. There is still hope to find your child's channel. How do we know? We listened to the young people. Nearly two-thirds of the young people who mentioned communication said, *I can tell her anything and she understands!*

How can you create clearer communication between the two of you?

WHAT'S A MOTHER TO DO?

Kids told us talk is not cheap in their book. Now they will let us know the qualities they appreciate and affirm in moms. We call these the channels to open up the "Talk from the Heart."

CHANNEL 1: UNDERSTANDING

We heard from a young person named Van earlier in *Dear*

Mom. Well, fifteen-year-old Van is back to emphasize a kid's need for understanding:

Thanks for always being there for me, Mom, and thanks for understanding.

Thirteen-year-old Tiffany jumps on Van's wagon by offering another insight to moms. She told us:

My relationship with my mom is a ten. We talk a lot. I can tell her anything. She will understand.

Can you see the hidden gem in her words? We talk a lot. That's a reference to time. Time not only boosts the quality of relationship, it also increases the quantity of exchange between mother and child. The more frequent the talk between Tiffany and her mom, the more opportunities her mom has to hear and understand Tiffany. The end result is a ten in Tiffany's mind. Guaranteed, Tiffany tells us, she will understand.

A Hebrew proverb states, "The purposes of a man's heart are deep waters, but a man of understanding draws them out."[1]

Remember, Mom, you can't control your child's desire to say anything and everything. But you can influence it by seeking to understand with every bit of energy you have. People are very tender creatures, children especially. When approached by a sincere person with a selfless motive expressed by the question, "How are you?," people often open up. When a listener responds, "I understand," and with empathy, humans unveil their hearts. When the heart is open, the relationship draws closer.

What does it mean to understand your child? Take the word apart: *under* and *stand.* Under defines position. To be under means to place yourself below your child. To stand means to come alongside and support or to lift up your child. When a mom goes down under, she places less priority on herself; she de-emphasizes the importance of getting her point across.

Sixteen-year-old Mitch offers what many women would consider to be a crowning commendation from their child. He says his relationship with his mom is a nine because . . .

We communicate very well. She is just so understanding of people.

Many of us moms (and dads, husbands, wives, children, employees, bosses) don't go "under" in relationships for fear of getting stepped on or tripped over and left behind, marred with dirt and heel marks. What about Mitch's mom? What color best describes his mom?

White. She is so generous and kind. She never puts herself before anyone.

Mitch's mom is white in her son's eyes—unblemished, clean, pure. She goes under in all she does.

A mom also has to fulfill the second part of the word understanding; she has to come alongside and support or lift up her child.

CHANNEL 2: SELF CONTROL

A second quality for solid communication between a mother and a child is mom's self-control. Another wise proverb states, "Whoever has no rule over his own spirit / Is like a city broken down, without walls."[2] To paraphrase the proverb, "A person without self-control is like a city without a police and fire department." When trouble comes, there is no one to rescue you.

One aspect of self-control means being yourself. A young man named Mickey has this to say about his mom:

She is the color blue. She has to be the calmest person in the world. If I could say anything to my mom, I would say, "Mom, you are the most understanding person in my house, but not the world."

Mom, be only what you can be, nothing else. Mickey's mom is very calm, the calmest in the world as far as he can see. But when it comes to understanding, she ranks top in her house; however, she does not take the gold in the entire universe.

There is a comical, insightful reality to Mickey's comment. Mom, you're great but not too great. Mom, you're the best in certain places, but not in every place. We find comforting freedom in his words. A source of self-control comes from a person's confidence. And confidence often comes from a realistic self-appraisal and therefore a willingness to say, "That's okay. I don't have to be all things to all people all the time. I can control my fears, my anxieties, my anger because I do not expect me to be more than I am."

Mom, you're loaded with purpose for your child. It will never be easy for you to say, "Oh sure, honey, whatever you would like to do with your life. I don't mind."

Forget it. You do mind. You mind because your child is always on your mind. So when unrealistic expectations come collapsing down on you, whether from your child, your husband, or the committee that meets in your head to pass on edicts to you, you're going to lose self-control unless you have the calm confidence that arises from a realistic self-appraisal. Twelve-year-old Kelly helps us underscore our point. She says:

My mom is the color blue. She is always calm, likely to understand me because she's a girl and had to go through the same stuff as me.

We don't know about you, but we don't hear Kelly saying her mom is a calm, cool bluelike water on the lake because she has mastered everything Kelly is going through. We hear Kelly saying, "My mom knows the pain and hassle of being a girl." There are just times when it's hard to be a young woman and Kelly's mom has been in that zone.

Is there enough self-control in your life for your child to select blue like Mickey and Kelly? Seventeen-year-old Brad says the same:

My mom is the color blue: cool and understanding.

We found most kids described mom's emotional state when they responded to our question about color. When it comes to communication, kids need calm moms. Unless a child perceives a women of self-control who knows her strengths and weaknesses, the child will not venture out into the depth of understanding.

The Websters Learn About Self-Control

Labor Day has always been a tough weekend for the Webster family. For five years running on Labor Day Weekend, we found ourselves moving back into our rented home we vacated over the summer. Finally we got the chance to move into a home of our own (okay, the bank's home) in 1994. Then Labor Day '94 came, and life moved out of our control.

Doug took our middle daughter, Jamie, to the doctor on Friday of the holiday weekend for her pre-elementary school physical. She's a healthy kid with a sharp mind, so we figured we would breeze right through. No such luck. Our wonderful pediatrician noticed Jamie's struggle seeing items on the eye chart with her left eye covered. A further exam revealed a spot in her eye. The doctor looked in her eye a few times, then looked back at Doug, then at Jamie again. In a solemn moment he said, "I see a spot in her eye. It's either a cataract or cancer."

Doug was stunned. Cataracts are for old people—and cancer?

"Would you be willing to see a specialist today if I can get you an appointment?" "Of course", Doug replied. No holiday for us that year. Once contacted, the pediatric opthamologist said over the phone, "It sounds very much like a cataract. Let's check first thing Tuesday morning."

We spent the weekend staring at our daughter, wondering, is it a cataract? What if it were cancer? In a *six-year-old*? It was a long, long weekend.

Over a year later, Jamie is thriving. A cataract surgeon removed her lens soon after the diagnosis proved the opthamologist right. Normally for adults with cataracts an artificial lens is implanted and the patient recovers with great success. Due to her age, Jamie will wait until her teenage years before she receives a replacement lens. For now, she lives with a contact in one eye, plus glasses. If you saw her, you would never know what she has been through. Her attitude is amazing. What an incredible kid she is. Still, every time we see her with glasses or with the patch she wears an hour a day over the good eye to strengthen the weaker eye, our hearts ache.

Self-control and emotional calm are extremely difficult to maintain when life's storms hit. How do moms know what to do or say? The key word here is know. Wisdom is another channel used to connect children with their mothers.

CHANNEL 3: WISDOM

When asked, "Mom, what do you think I should do?" a wise woman knows what to say. Her advice is timely, accurate, and effective. A few young people referred to this:

My relationship with my mom is a ten. I can tell her anything. She's always been there for me during tough times and gives great advice.
Holly, nineteen years old

My relationship with my mom is a nine. I know I can tell her anything and she won't judge me. [She's] always willing to listen and give me good advice.
Stephanie, seventeen years old

Both of these young women believe they have wise moms. Their relationships rank near or at the top. Stephanie and Holly can tell their moms anything. They both apply the word always when they refer to their mothers. They both say that during the tough times, when they tell everything and run the risk of judgment, their moms listen, stay close, and offer advice that is deemed "good" by these girls. Mom, what does it take to reach a point where your daughter or son is ready to receive your advice willingly and even label it "good"? Take the course we heard kids lay out for moms:

1. Always be there, but don't always be there.
   (Interpretation: Stay close but don't control.)
2. Be a selfless, affirming, calm mom, both understanding and self-controlled.
3. Listen, don't judge. (We'll discuss judgment in the next chapter.)
4. Now, advise.

How do we know we have what it takes to offer advice that will be labeled as good?"

Wisdom Found

Mom, are you willing to invest your valuable resources to become wiser? As another proverb states, "Search for it like hidden treasure." [1]

Is wisdom a pearl of great price, prompting you to take all you have and sell it to buy a field in which the prize is buried? We want to draw your attention to a fantastic best-seller. (No, not Dear Dad but we appreciate the thought.) The Bible. It is the best-selling book in the history of humankind. We recommend it highly. Really, it is quite a bargain because you get sixty-six books all wrapped under one cover. If you are not too familiar with the material, you will be delighted to see how insightful it really is about parenting, marriage, money, and all the other "biggies" that hit moms on a daily basis. You will find experiences, both good and bad, of countless other humans from which you can draw much wisdom and insight. Behind the entire "what" of wisdom found in this book of books, you are guided along the way by the "who" of God as the author and perfecter of wisdom. You will even notice the entire second half, what is called the "New" section, has the God/man of history, Jesus of Nazareth, as the central character around which all of the writings revolve.

You will be amazed as you learn wisdom from the pages and the presence of God and His word. It's proven true for ages and it still works today.

In Appendix B, you will find a list of other books that we believe contain some valuable elements of practical wisdom for your role as a mother. They are not divinely written, but many are divinely influenced. They will prove true as solid sources for the mom who wants wisdom for herself and her family.

One last encouragement pertaining to wisdom found: the value of wisdom modeled. Is there an individual or group of women from whom you draw support, guidance, shared experiences, and simple encouragement?

Robin has been involved in an organization called MOPS—Mothers of Pre-Schoolers—for the past five years. MOPS is a moms organization based in Colorado with chapters throughout the United States and various other countries. Robin's group is affiliated with our home church in southern

California, Coast Hills Community Church. From nearly the beginning of our church's existence, MOPS has served the mothers of young children throughout our community.

"We anticipate the weekly involvement of three hundred women this year in our church alone," Robin says. "I do not know of a more effective, encouraging, and exciting effort to help us moms survive and succeed. The weekly meetings offer moms a chance to spend time with another adult, eat great food, learn crafts, and glean insights from speakers on various topics. All the while our children enjoy the care and guidance of a top-notch program for kids.

"I have participated as a speaking leader for the past four years. The privilege and responsibility of finding and sharing wisdom for moms is one of my greatest joys in life. In the past few years, Doug and I have teamed up to do "MOPS and Pops" nights for the women and their spouses or boyfriends. (Doug likes to call the guys FLOPS: Fathers Living with Pre-Schoolers.)"

Local MOPS groups have exploded across the country in the past few years. Why? Moms need and desperately want help. If you feel the same, you are not alone. Mom, who can give you the support, education, and mentoring you need to survive as a mom, especially if you're a working and/or single parent? We highly recommend finding a MOPS group in your area. Call your local church or contact MOPS in Colorado at 1311 South Clarkson, Denver, CO 80210 (303) 733-5353.

Our last stop on the wisdom trail will help you tune in to hear your child's heart.

Fifteen-year-old Erika told us:

My relationship with my mom is an eight. We have a good relationship but sometimes she just doesn't understand my views.

Eleven-year-old Ariel said:

My relationship with my mom is a nine. Sometimes she understands and sometimes she doesn't.

What happens when you strive to understand, control yourself, and seek wise ways of relating, and still your relationship encounters the gaps that Erika and Ariel refer to? What happens when wisdom applied appears to be wisdom denied?

Wise moms learn the difference between a simple misunderstanding and the inability to understand each other at all.

Misunderstanding.   When a mom is sincerely trying to understand and she misinterprets what is said, she misses the bull's-eye. Mom is saying, "I want to understand, I just don't think I get it."

What can mom do? Speak from the heart. Say, "Erika, I am trying to understand you. Will you help me? Would you be willing to use different words to help me better understand what you are saying? I am trying." Mom missed but she is aiming as straight as possible.

An inability to understand.   After a diligent effort by mom or both mom and child, mom's wisdom tells her they do not have the ability to understand each other. Something is getting in the way and neither of them can see it. A wise mom will respond, "I am trying and I have tried to understand you. My goal is a ten on the scale, but we keep missing something. I may need a third party to better help me understand what you are trying to communicate." At that point Mom, you need a person who can see what you two can't see. You can recruit dad, a mutual friend, a pastor, or a professional counselor. Don't give up. Call for assistance to help your child and you reach mutual understanding.

Other times moms may choose to not understand.

Deciding to not understand. This last phase sounds like a complete contradiction to what we have been positing through this entire chapter. Yet you may decide that mom's understanding is not essential for the situation. There are certain times when mom needs to say, "I don't understand, but I do not think I need to understand. This is for you to work out on your own. I am committed to you, but I either can't understand or I will only complicate things if I try to stay close. It's time for you to set sail on your own with this one. I am choosing to stay on shore and keep you in mind without keeping you in control." In other words, it is a time to place more value on release than understanding.

What happens when a mom dials in to her child's station? The strong communication opens the way for other vital aspects of a mother/child relationship.

As the trip continues, somewhere along the ride or as the young adult leaves the family trip, he or she broadcasts the final *Dear Mom* message loud and clear, well within the reach of mom's receiver. They say, *Mom, I love you and I appreciate everything you do!* (The topic of Chapter 10.)

What happens when relational static distorts the connection between mom and child? What if mom disregards understanding, denies self-control, and degrades wisdom? She unplugs the mother/child relationship.

In the next chapter, we will meet kids who experience the other three types of communication:

- *I can tell you almost anything.*
- *I can't tell you everything.*
- *I can't tell you anything.*

Dear Mom,

I can say anything to you. I know you will understand, you won't get mad, and if I need it, you'll have wise advice for me. Thanks for always being there so I can really let you know all about my life.

With Love,
Your child

CHAPTER 5

Dear Mom,

 I can't tell you anything.

Love,
Your child

I CAN'T TELL
YOU ANYTHING.

I don't always tell her everything.
Lisa, fourteen years old

I can tell her how I feel or almost anything else.
Raymond, thirteen years old

*My relationship with my mom is a three. She doesn't listen very well,
she judges me, and she is way too over protective.*
Ken, sixteen years old

Awhile back Doug received a phone call from a youth worker, one of those brave, rare, under-recognized and over-worked persons or "para-parents" as we call them. They come alongside youth and their families to fight off the barrage of social bombs blasting families today. Most are volunteers and the few who are paid receive little compensation.

The youth worker told Doug that a frantic parent had received some startling information from her teenage daughter who had just returned from a youth group event. The teenager told her mom she had engaged in sexual activity during the outing. The mom was appalled. How could the leaders have allowed such a thing to take place? (The rendezvous for the teenage tryst took place late at night while the rest of the campers were fast asleep.) And why, she asked, would the group let another teenager of such obvious low morals attend the retreat? The youth worker was caught off guard and he called Doug for an objective perspective.

Let us pause to mention here that we are champions for chastity—a difficult but feasible accomplishment even in today's sex-minded culture. When it comes to sex, females face the greatest consequences, far outreaching the impact on young men.

Doug's first response was to empathize with the mother. Young people make decisions of which the consequences will stay with them the rest of their lives. Doug then proceeded to point out how important it is for the mom to realize the candid nature of her relationship with her teenager. Believe me, most kids don't come home and share stories about sex. Like one of the young people we met said to us:

I can tell my mom everything except things about the opposite sex.

(Is it any surprise this came from a fifteen-year-old who chose to remain anonymous?)

Now, returning to the young woman who told her mother the truth about the youth outing. Yes, the information is disheartening and shocking to mom. But the child still spoke up. That kind of *I can tell my mom anything* level of communication is uncommon. When sex surfaces, most people duck 'n cover. Whatever the mom and teenager had going to this point was unique and valuable. What mom does from here on out will determine whether or not the teenager keeps the communication lines open.

The youth worker and Doug talked about mom's opportunity to educate the teenager on the consequences of sexual activity. Mom also needed to communicate her spiritual and relational values regarding sex. The two talked about encouraging mom to be clear with her thoughts and feelings without blasting the bridges of communication she had worked so hard to establish. A sleeping bag encounter is no matter to doze over, but it's not worth bulldozing mom's decade of building. They talked about trust: between mom and child, youth worker and mom, child and partner, and child and God.

Mom, what would you do if you found yourself on the receiving end of such a heart-to-heart talk with your teen? This chapter looks at the large number of moms who may never know what their child did last Saturday night at 1:15 A.M. The good news is: Mom, you'll never know what went wrong. The bad news is: You'll never be able to guide your child before he or she hits the next right or wrong fork in the road.

We want to take a look at the other three levels of communication in a mother/child relationship:

- *Mom, I can tell you almost anything.*
- *Mom, I can't tell you everything.*
- Mom, I can't tell you anything.

After a brief understanding of the differences in mother/child communication levels, you will discover six obstacles that get in the way of clear communication. Once the obstacles are identified, we can ask, "What's a mother to do?"

THREE LEVELS OF COMMUNICATION

- *Mom, I can tell you almost anything.*

As we poured through the comments from hundreds of young people, we noticed that many kids indicated a possible "ten" relationship, and then add, one word: *almost*. These kids can tell mom just about everything. The following young people rated their relationships with their moms either a seven or an eight. They said:

> *I can tell her anything (almost). She is also fun.*
> Kelly, twelve years old

> *I can talk to her about almost anything.*
> Marvin, eighteen years old

> *We're really close, but there are just some things I can't talk to her about.*
> Ragan, fifteen years old

Even our anonymous friend who can talk about everything but the opposite sex gave mom an eight on the scale.

One young girl named Sonia said:

There are certain things I feel I can't tell my mom. She pretty much knows everything.

"Pretty much," she said, but not everything. Sonia has her mental list of dos and don'ts.

What happens if mom does get the whole scoop from the child?

I could tell her anything, but I choose not to. A ten would mean I did.

He confirms our theory. If you get a ten, Mom, it means you know it all. Does it make you wonder what behavior or thought is tucked away in your child's "confidential" file, far away from mom's view? Some moms don't even hear most of what's on the heart of their child. Two more levels of communication exist between the mother and child:

- *Mom, I can't tell you everything.*

Notice the negative twist to this message. A positive comment says, "Mom, you hear nearly everything that's on my heart." This negative comment says, "Mom, there are some things on my heart you will never hear."

But it gets worse! One last level remains:

- *Mom, I can't tell you anything.*

When young people say this, they are often thinking what fourteen-year-old Katie told us:

It's hard for me to open up to her like I could when I was little. Ever since I entered high school she is the parent, the one making the rules and not my friend.

If I could say anything to my mom, I would tell her about my life when I'm not home: the guys I like, the Bible study I'm going to on Saturday nights, my first kiss, my first heart break, my friends. It's like she doesn't even want to listen anymore or maybe I just can't talk to her anymore.

What hinders young people from doing what seems so important to them, telling mom all? As we listen to young people, we find three reasons mom doesn't know the whole story: the child's action, the child's choice, and the mom's action.

The child's action.   The child knows that his action violates mom's value system so the child prefers to keep mom in the dark. These young people reinforce cliches such as "Ignorance is bliss" or "What you don't know won't hurt you." The child is saying, "Mom, if you knew, I could be in big trouble. I'd just as soon keep you ignorant and happy."

Fourteen-year-old Sam said:

I've tried things I wasn't supposed to.

Sam doesn't tell all because he has done certain things he knows his mother will object to.

The child's choice.   This second reason why mom doesn't know the whole story is an extension of the first: It is the child's choice. When a child chooses not to inform or involve mom, the mother can do very little to change the situation. If mom knows about the behavior but can't get a verbal confirmation (or confession) from the child, the mother is left with the option to either drop the case or become a private investigator. (If only TV would create a new show called *PI Mom: Angela Lansbury Meets 911*.) A child may choose to take the fifth amendment and not speak up. Some kids just have some feelings or thoughts they don't want to share. Don't we all. The situation often drives mom to her strongest, stealth weapon: her intuition. Don't be surprised, Mom, if your child knows that you want to know and the child uses this to his or her advantage. When we asked one seventeen-year-old to say anything to mom, the student responded:

Hi, Mom. I'm having kids!

After a pregnant pause, the young person said, *just kidding*. Many kids know just how long to stall before unveiling the truth, much like the time gap between a parachuter's free fall and his timely arrival on the ground. Kids keep the truth packed away behind their backs long enough for mom to panic over the fast-approaching, hard stop of reality. Then they pull the JK cord. *Just kidding*.

The third reason for the child/mother barrier is mom's action.

Mom's action. Sometimes the last person a child wants to talk to is an aggressive mom in hot pursuit of truth and justice. Although not exhaustive, we offer six blocks to your child's heart: embarrassment, disrespect, uncommonality, judgment, displeasure (a displeased or unsatisfied mom), and anger. The sixth block, anger, is so significant, we have dedicated Chapter 7 to it.

FIVE BLOCKS TO COMMUNICATION

Block 1: Embarrassment

One young person unveils the first block to open mother/child communication:

I can talk to my mom about almost everything. In public she can sometimes embarrass me.

When a mom takes what is shared in private and goes public with it, few kids want to hang around. Their embarrassment teaches them, "Never tell Mom anything I don't want shared over the loud speaker at Wal-Mart." In such a situation, Mom may be inclined to say, "Oh, come on, sweetie, it's not that bad."

Look again, Mom, it *is* that bad. Embarrassment, like other feelings, is not easily diagnosed from afar. What is not embarrassing to you may be totally embarrassing to your child. Also remember a young person's social standing in the commonwealth of childhood friendships is the only currency a child possesses. Acceptance is his or her credit line. You are in deep trouble with nothing left but to be banished to the dark, outer regions of your child's life if you are in the mall and you say something like, "Look, Katie, there is Kevin. Hiiiii Kevinnnn! Katie, isn't that the boy you like? Kevin, come over here and say hello to us."

Bite your lip if you need to. It will be worth the pain. It works for eighteen-year-old Maureen and her mom. She rates the relationship a ten because . . .

I can tell her anything and I do. She can tell me anything and we're not embarrassed.

Block 2: Disrespect

Robin remembers a time a few years back when she was having a difficult day in her role as mom. "I realized Attila the Hun had nothing on me that day. I was ruling the house with an iron fist. Something snapped me into reality. I became aware of who my children are and how I was treating them, and the two didn't match up. To remind myself, I placed a note on each of my two daughters' bedroom doors. The notes read:

TREAT BROOKELYN WITH RESPECT.
TREAT JAMIE WITH RESPECT.

"These notes became a constant reminder of how I was to treat them. I found myself asking, 'How would I want to be treated if I were in their shoes?' It shaped the way I disciplined them. Respect did not remove the need to discipline. It just meant disciplining them without demeaning them. I was challenged to treat them with honor."

In the language of today's young people, "Mom, don't *dis* me." (Next time you hear that statement, you'll know what they mean.)

Not long ago Doug was speaking to a group of parents of special needs children. The issue at hand was the challenge of keeping a marriage vibrant and alive when a couple is raising a child with special needs. During a very heart-wrenching question-and-answer session one man asked Doug, "What one thing can we do to make sure our marriage stays alive and well?"

Doug responded, "In a word, respect. Robin and I have built our marriage of thirteen years with this one mutually agreeable value: We will respect each other. We don't always like each other, but we always respect each other. If the respect is ever violated, the partner is free to bring the issue up immediately. There are no ifs, ands, or buts when it comes to respect."

The bedrock of any healthy relationship is respect for the individual. Respect dis-allows certain behavior, dialogue, or thoughts. John Trent and Gary Smalley call it *honor*, a way to treasure what is most important to you. Does your child notice when you respect someone enough to treasure them? Trent and Smalley write, "With their fine-tuned radar system, a child picks up whether he is more valuable to you than your property or projects."[1]

Like a guardsman at a castle gate, respect serves to protect a couple or family from life-threatening attacks of dishonor. Once the shield of respect is torn down, the armies of relational atrophy will march on the unfortunate inhabitants and virtually burn, loot, and destroy everyone. No prisoners will be taken. Only a cloud of past memories will remain.

What happens when mom's action communicates disrespect to her child? It disrupts communication. If fifteen-year-old Ryan could say anything to his mom, he would say:

Just be how you are because I like how you are, but sometimes you need to respect my feelings.

Ryan is not asking for a superwoman or even a super change from his mom. His straightforward request is for respect. We heard what Ryan was saying. Now, Mom, listen to what we think he means:

Mom, be who you are because that is who I like. My only request is you offer the same to me. Allow me to be who I am and to feel how I feel. When you do, I take that to mean you want me to be who I am because that's who you like!

Mom, be on guard against the arrows of dishonor or you'll have mutiny in the camp.

Block 3: Uncommonality

Here is one of the most peculiar statements we heard from anyone:

We like the same types of music, clothes, and sometimes even guys. We really understand each other.
Emily, twelve years old

We're not sure what the guys part means. This may be one of those highly liberated mother/daughter relationships. We can see it now on the next talk show . . . "Women who date their twelve-year-old daughter's friends."

Let's assume (or at least hope) Emily is referring to mom's innocent comments such as, "Oh, I think he is cute also." Beyond that issue, we know you are probably thinking, "Yeah, right. Just wait until little Emily reaches thirteen. She won't even want to consider herself a female if it means being in the same gender as her mother." Let us offer some hope from thirteen-year-old Alexa:

My mom and I talk about everything. We relate to each other a lot. We have a lot in common.

We have a niece named Alexa who has a great mom in Doug's sister Jana. It is a joy to watch the two of them develop in the early years what will be so vital in the teenager years, a mother and daughter's ability to talk because they can relate. They share common interests such as swimming, an appreciation for casual clothes, an unrelenting craving for chocolate, and even the days when they both, in the words of Jana, "go hormonal as women do."

We hope in eight yeas from now when our niece is in her early teens, she too will say, "I can tell my mom anything because we can relate." What does it mean to relate? It means to share. It means to have common experiences, interests, and/or viewpoints. Moms who lack commonality with their children will stumble over a major block in communication.

Have you ever tried to converse with complete stranger who speaks another language? Until you find a common means of language (often hand gestures) or a shared experience, you are left with nothing but two people smiling and nodding. Funny how universal a smile is. Too many mothers and children are like strangers serendipitously linked in a foreign land, minus the smiling.

Block 4: Judgment

It is time for Alexa to speak again. Actually, this is a different Alexa than the thirteen-year-old mentioned earlier. This Alexa gives her relationship with her a mom a seven and a half. Her comments are not quite so inspiring. She said:

I love my mom a lot. Sometimes I just feel like I can't tell her too much about my life, or she'll use it against me at a later date.

One phrase comes to mind: The Miranda Act. Think of the bazillion TV cop shows we have all seen too much of and recall this statement: "You have the right to remain silent. You have the right to an attorney. If you cannot afford one, one will be appointed to you. And *anything you say can be used against you in a court of law.*"

TV criminals at least get a public defender. The kid in the family court is left to represent herself. Mom, we are not asking questions about right and wrong. We are talking about a child's perception of her mom as a woman with a judgmental, "three strikes, you're out," jail-filling agenda. You better believe the child will stay quiet. Judgment is the most ominous, shadow-casting, hope-stealing block to ever enter a relationship.

Mom, would you be willing to consider a courageous assessment? Imagine a courtroom setting and list out the various players: judge, prosecuting attorney, defending attorney, bailiff, stenographer, news reporter, supportive family member. Then ask your child to select the role that best describes you. You may be intrigued. You may be depressed. You may become angry and judgmental. But you will most likely unveil a new piece of evidence.

What may happen if mom retains the role of judge or jury? A rating of seven may seem like a gold medal compared to what some kids say about their moms. Just ask this sixteen-year-old girl who said:

My relationship with my mom is a three. She doesn't listen very well, she judges me, and she's way too over protective. What would I say if I could say anything? You mean if my mom actually listened to me and didn't judge me for what I was thinking? If you would be more understanding and helpful we could get along better.

Unending judgment wears people down. Her mom, like too many moms, will find herself asking, "What happened to our relationship? How did we end up at a three?"

Mom, when you look for the block of judgment, do you see it shaking its long, bony finger right at you? Judgment and criticism will put your relationship with your child in the tank.

Block 5: Displeasure

The simple statement "If mamma ain't happy, ain't nobody happy" is actually quite profound. A mother's happiness is often an emotional barometer in the home. Mom, are you pleased with your child? Do your children know that you are happy with who they are, how they live, how well they perform? Don't answer too quickly. A simple oversight can block the heart of a child. This fifth block is the block of displeasure: when mom is not pleased or when mamma ain't happy.

How do we know it is important for a child to please a

mom? Think about the victorious athletes who appear on television after a successful football, basketball, or baseball game. The huge, 200-pound, seven foot man waves his index finger symbolizing number one and then says, "Hi Mom!"

It doesn't matter if dad was the head coach, drove junior to every practice, stayed up late watching the opposition's game films, paid extra cash to get those "gotta have 'em" shoes, ate lousy hot dogs and stale popcorn washed down by flat, warm, diet soda, and attended games come rain or shine. When all is said and done, the winning athlete says, "Hi Mom!" Sometime it's just not fair (Doug's comment.)

Why? Kids want mom to be happy—happy with life and pleased with them. When asked what she would say if she could say anything, thirteen-year-old Lindsay said:

Because I get As in school, doesn't mean I can get As at home.

It is one thing to flunk algebra. Imagine flunking home room and we mean the real home room. Mom, here is the bottom-line question: Do your kids measure up to your expectations? They want to know before they let you know what they know. Does that mean mom is always bright, cheery, happy, and pleased? By all means, no! Does that mean mom can never have higher expectations for her child? Of course not. The more central question is do your children know how high, how often, how much you hope for them?

One of the greatest challenges we face in our marriage, let alone our parenting, is agreeing upon a clear and solid understanding of each other's expectations. Some of our best conflicts come from misunderstood or misappropriated expectations. It is extremely difficult to meet unknown or unstated expectations. In the Webster family, we are doing the best we can to never take responsibility for what we were not told. It's hard enough to fulfill the stuff we know about, let alone live telepathically.

Mom, ask yourself these three questions:

1. Are my expectations clear in the mind of my child?
2. Does my child have the resources (time, money, help) to fulfill my expectations?
3. Are my expectations fair and reasonable to match the age or ability of my child?

Mom, this is tough stuff. A woman whose happiness is dependent upon her child's ability to fulfill her expectations makes for a very vulnerable person. Your child will fail you. Your husband, your friends, your parents, your health, your money will fail you. That's just part of living with people who are human. (Remember, you will also fail them at times.)

Mom, if your expectations are not posted, your child will not enjoy a long, comfortable ride with you.

We will discuss the sixth block to communication—anger—in Chapter 7. For now, let's look at how a mom can overcome these first five blocks.

WHAT'S A MOTHER TO DO?

Mom, it's time to devise a plan to blast open these blocks

to the heart. Believe it or not, some kids are even devising their own plans. Thirteen-year-old Nicki said:

If I could say anything to my mom, I would say, "I'll always be there. My plan is to show you that I understand."

Mom, like Nicki, make it your mission to grow closer to your children by always being there when they need you (but not there when they don't). Here are some beginning stepping stones:

1. Make Room.

Your child is growing up. He or she is facing new experiences, emotions, and thoughts never encountered before. Listen carefully to your child for he or she might have something to stay like twelve-year-old Kelly:

Mom, I'm at an age where life is difficult to understand and I feel a lot of pressure. Stop treating me as a kid.

Give your child room to grow. Few parents anticipate boundary adjustment when the child hits the early teen years. Mom, allow for misunderstandings. Give your child the time to choose when, where, and how much information he or she will let you know, unless, of course, there is a life-threatening situation. If not, give your kid living space.

On a practical level, ask yourself, "What one area of action or decision have I expanded for my child in the past year?" Some adjustments are obvious such as obtaining a driver's license or moving from junior high to high school. The areas of communication are more difficult to identify. When your eleven-year-old daughter says about a boy, "He is neat," you as a mom think, *The boy is a nice friend*. When the same daughter says the same line about a boy three years later, you think, *The boy will never be allowed near my daughter again* or maybe a variation thereof.

Take a look at the following list of topics and estimate how much room your child thinks she or he has. If you are really brave, ask your child to answer for himself/herself and then compare your answers.

- dating
- the opposite sex
- sex
- grades
- money
- politics
- religion
- others you can add

Mom, success and an improved rating may be as close as your willingness to let your child move away.

2. Act Like You Mean It

When you have worked to open the channels and clear away the blocks or static in the radio broadcast, is your job finished? Not quite yet. Now comes time for mom to act like she means it. Two more action steps exist for you, Mom, if you want to move your communication with your child toward a higher number on the relationship scale. Step number one: *invite*. Step number two: *initiate*.

What do you do if your child does not want to talk with you? *Invite your child to a closer relationship with you.* Speak in the first person, using "I" language not "you" words. Say something like: "I want to know you better. I would love to hear more about you—your dreams, your fears, your thoughts. I will never force you to tell me, but I will always be there to hear you. I'm working as hard as I can to keep the channels open and remove any obstacles standing in the way between us. When you're ready to talk, I'm ready to listen."

What else can you do with a child who's not talking? *Initiate.* Mom, more is caught than taught. If you want to draw closer to your child, or any relationship for that matter, initiate the closeness. Model what it means to tell someone more about you than they already know. Don't overwhelm your child with all the dirt, all the hopes, every bit of intimacy. Remember, your child is your child—not your spouse, not an adult, not your counselor. He or she is younger than you, so appropriate the level of unloading you do with your child. (There is time for a second helping when the timing is right.) But let your child know you trust him or her with what's most near and dear to you.

Trust is a delicate item to be handled with care. Sabrina told us:

My relationship with my mom is a seven. I can't trust her and she can't trust me.

For families like Sabrina's, trust needs to be rebuilt. Mom, your initiative may be just the leap of faith the relationship needs to move out of the "stuck on seven" and climb toward a towering ten. You may find yourself in a family like Mickey's, a fifteen-year-old young man who rated his relationship with his mom a nine. He spoke with dignity when he said:

My mom trusts me not to tell anybody else what she told me.

We encourage you to find an area of your life and extend it to your child. You can go back to the list we used earlier and pick a topic that fits. And if your child shares one of these topics with you, try not to reply, "I knew it" or "I told you so." If you need to let him or her know how important it is to you, talk from your heart again. You may soon find your child offering back to you more than you ever thought you would know.

What if you have done all you can do and your child *still* chooses to stay at bay? There is one more thing you can do: wait patiently.

3. Wait Patiently

Impatience will be the Kryptonite of the twenty-first century. We live in a world moving too quickly to develop intimate relationships. High speed global travel, technological equipment in offices and homes, satellite communication, and instant visual media imaging support the statement, "It's a small world." Speed and efficiency outweigh quality and effectiveness. Our weakness of impatience will be much like Superman's demise from his Achilles' heel, Kryptonite. Slowly and subtly, we humans run the risk of not waiting long enough to find success. We drive by too quickly to capture the broadcast of the nearby radio station.

Not long ago our friends helped us celebrate the planting and growing of our new backyard by giving us a yard party. People brought flowers, plants, bushes, and even money to go toward our future plans for sod. One dear friend, Sherri, commented after her husband dropped off two big bags of fertilizer, "You know we're close friends when we give you two bags of cow poop as a gift." Ah, the aroma of friendship as it fills the air!

One couple, Barbara and John, was delighted to hear of the yard party and excited to help celebrate us moving into our new home. They have been long-standing friends and incredible supporters of our endeavors to help young families over the past fourteen years. As a family of six with all four children out of high school, they are also a beacon of light and proof to us that a family can make it through the era of adolescence and survive intact.

Barbara told Doug she had some extra plants she would like to give us. When Doug first saw the greenery that evening, it was difficult to make out sizes and types. Out of ignorance, Doug said, "Can I say yes to your offer and take one of each?"

Barbara bestowed two plants of each species on us, and Doug and Barbara's son, Tim, carefully loaded them into the Webster van. Since Robin is the yard mastermind and Doug is the unpaid, hired hand, Doug decided to let Robin choose what to do with the gifts.

Later we learned one of the plants was a sago palm. The

plant was small for a palm, no higher than three feet. Its frawns were miserably prickly as Doug had realized in transit. It looked nice once we set it on the back patio, but to be honest, we were not sure what to do with it. Then friends, neighbors, and family began to comment on the sago. "Wow, what a beautiful sago! Do you know how long it takes for one of those to grow to that size?" "Oh, that is beautiful. We just bought one about six-inches tall, and it cost us nearly fifty dollars. That's an incredible palm."

The more we heard about the life of a sago, the more we understood the value of that small palm. What takes a long time to develop, even though it may seem small and prickly to the ignorant eye, can be very valuable, expensive, and rare.

To be honest, we love the sago, but we doubt we would have bought a small one at eight dollars per inch with hopes of someday having the beautiful palm adorning our back patio. Fortunately for us, Barbara has more patience, more wisdom, and more generosity than the average friend.

Mom, when you've done all you can do, don't do anything. Wait patiently for your child to respond. Remember, patience is inactive, but it is not passive. Patience says, "You can do it. I have enough hope for both of us to share, and besides, you and the end result are worth the wait."

Eighteen-year-old Laurie and her mom are just beginning to understand what is meant by the cliche, "Good things come to those who wait." Laurie reminds all of us—regardless of our age—that there is hope:

My relationship with my mom is an eight. It's getting better. It used to be a six. Now that I am an adult, I can understand her more. What would I say if I could say anything to my mom? Mom, sorry about those difficult teenage years. Your patience has made me a strong and capable adult.

Mom, you may have to invest a great deal of time weeding, watering, and watching. You may find yourself up to your elbows in cow poop. Will it pay off? The Hebrew proverb answers that question. It says, "Train up a child in the way he should go, / And when he is old he will not depart from it."[2]

A WORD FOR MOMS WHO HEAR WHAT THEY DON'T WANT TO HEAR

Before we end the chapter, we want to offer two particular thoughts. First, we don't want you to close *Dear Mom* thinking your child has carte blanche to say or do anything.

Secondly, we want to offer some hope and insight for moms with kids in crisis. An adult who is striving to build an open, close relationship with kids may succeed, and then end up receiving very serious information. One mother recently discovered her child had been involved in illegal drug use. The child was afraid of what his parents would do. Another mom told us how her step-children told her things they didn't want their dad to know. She asked, "What do I do or say when my step-child comes to me and says, 'I am not going to be around on Saturday because I will be with Mom. Promise you won't tell Dad'?"

Remember the mom who called the youth worker with

startling news about her child's sexual encounter? The answer is still the same. First it is important to recognize the risk the child is taking and to appreciate the child's honesty. Moms need to build a bridge for further trust by acknowledging and affirming their child. And remember, it is likely the child is just uncovering a small portion of the disaster. Your child may be like the kid who dumps a gallon of milk on the kitchen floor and bellows out, "Mommy, I just spilled a little milk." Mom can count on the accuracy of two words: *spilled* and *milk*. The word *just* is questionable, and almost always the description *little* is severely understated.

Mom, if you hear your child say, "I was at a party and I drank a beer," this may be the truth, the whole truth, and nothing but the truth. Or it may be a version of the truth. Yes, the teen went to the party and drank a beer. But the student also went to a few other parties and drank a few more beers. It's possible the teen rode in a car with a driver under the influence of alcohol. Many kids send trial balloons into the sky to test the weather before they unleash the entire fleet.

The second challenge at a time such as this is self-control. It's hard not to fly off the handle: "I can't believe you would do something so stupid. Do you ever listen to what your father and I tell you?" Mom, if you think it, you're normal. (If you don't even think it, you may need more help than your kid.) If you say it, you're average. Just think before you speak.

Assuming you've done these things, the third step is to offer your support. Something as simple as, "I'm here with you. We will get through this together." Those of us who have spent a career working with young people realize a young person in trouble needs an adult who will ride out the storm. Adolescents who make it to age twenty and survive adolescence are not perfect kids; instead they are real kids whose parents (or other adults) have been committed to their survival and success.

The Queen Elizabeth II recently survived a tidal wave. Experts estimated the wave was ninety-five feet high because the top of the monstrous wall of water reached the bridge where the captain and the crew were steering the ship. The captain said he saw the wave coming their way. He slowed the boat down from twenty-five knots to five knots and steered straight into that huge wave. At first there was a large shudder. Then smaller shudders. The final damage was just a few bent railings and some chipped paint. Hard to believe, but most of the ship's passengers slept through the event!

Batten down the hatches, Mom. If you're in for a stormy ride, the best thing to do is to go straight through it. It may be prudent to slow down your family's speed. Get all hands on deck. Act as if you (and your husband) are the captain, and you will stay as long as you can help keep things afloat. (The notion of going down with the ship is a noble thought for movies and memoirs of Victory at Sea, but not parenting.) With the support and guidance of the experienced captain, the Queen Elizabeth II survived the tidal wave. Many families have done the same.

After you have affirmed the child's character, controlled your self and offered your support, take the final step: commit to truth and healing. Tell your child you will do whatever you can to help the child face the truth and find healing. Drinking a beer at a party or sneaking around behind dad's back to visit mom are symptoms of something bigger.

Kids drink because their souls are thirsty. If their bodies were thirsty, they would drink soda, water, or juice. Few kids we know like the taste of beer. Wine coolers and various other mixed drinks taste better, but few teenagers really want a Bud to quench their thirst. They are searching for a real buddy or acceptance into a peer group. And kids who sneak around dad to visit mom are really desiring to continue to be with mom, even though dad and mom are apart. The dad may be expecting the child to hate his ex-wife as much as he does. Or he may be trying to protect his child from mom's illegal or unsafe lifestyle.

Look for the problem and then expect healing. Mom, when you commit to your child, you are seeking truth—not blind allegiance. A child caught in unhealthy living based on falsehood will expect you to act according to his values. Don't buy in when a child says, "Promise you won't tell anybody." It is not a formula for healing, it is a prescription for disaster, yours included. Compare the child's request to a passenger on the boat begging the captain to turn the ship sideways to try to outrun the tidal wave. That's why inexperienced, rookie shipmates don't make captains. For the same reason, we refer parenthood to adults. Parenting deserves a NC-17 label (no children under age seventeen). The teenage pregnancy crisis not only damages young people today and burdens our social systems with impoverished families, it places the difficult task of parenting into the hands of young, immature, pre-adults. Teenage parenting is like giving the helm of the Queen

Elizabeth II to a first time kayak rower. Maturity and wisdom are prerequisites for steering kids straight through the storms of life.

What does a mom say to a child who says, "Promise not to tell"? Here is what we suggest: "I will support you and you can trust me. I will do whatever I can to find truth and healing for you. But I will not promise to not tell. That's not in your best interest."

In other words, Mom, you are saying, "I will not lie or act against your healing. I will not lessen my character or lower our family's values to support you being a character." Yes, you may shut down the communication line, but that is out of your control. Your move is to go back to inviting, initiating, and removing blocks.

One last bit of guidance for moms who hear too much: call for help. Mom, your first and best step is to kneel before God. Call on God when you need a power source bigger than your problem. Countless numbers of people have survived the storm with His guidance, His truth, His healing—and the calm He can bring to a storm. You may also need to rally some of the people God has placed directly in your life. Pastors, counselors, and friends who are either professionally educated or personally experienced. Mom, you're not alone with your child. Don't act like it.

Life is a phone call. Some moms wish they never answered. Other moms wish they would get more calls and remove the almosts and nevers that clog the communication lines between them and their children. Wise moms believe their child could tell them anything if they chose to. What happens with moms who are always there in a positive, balanced way? In a simple kid cliche, they say, *We get along*. The next chapter will focus on kids who told us: "Mom and I are friends because we get along so well."

Dear Mom,

I have a hard time talking with you. I can't say every-thing to you, and sometimes I can't say anything at all without you judging me or getting mad at me. If I could, I would tell you everything that goes through my head, all the questions and feelings that swamp my mind.

With Love,
Your child

CHAPTER 6

> *Dear Mom,*
>
> *We get along.*
>
> *Love,*
>
> *Your child*

WE GET ALONG.

My relationship with my mom is a ten. We always get along and we are very close.

Mike, thirteen years old

White goes with every color, and my mom gets along with everyone. She is a friendly person. I share almost everything with her, and we are friends.

Anonymous

Mom, I love you so much. You are my best friend. I can always count on you. You're the greatest person in the world.

Krista, fourteen years old

One of the benefits of Robin's mom being a young mom was that it was a little more natural to get along and be friends with a woman who was not much more than twenty years older than her.

"I was the third of three children, and my mom was twenty-one years old when I was born. I can distinctly remember celebrating my mom's thirtieth birthday. In contrast, I was thirty-one when our first child was born and thirty-six when my third child was born. My mom released the kids into the world as adults and still had some time ahead of her. Sometimes

I wonder if I'll live to see my last child, Chase, graduate from high school! I'll be the one in the wheelchair with the camera.

"Late nights when the rest of the family would go to bed were prime times for my relationship with mom. The rush of the day would disappear into a quiet calm. We developed what I call the 'safe zone' where each of us could say what was on our minds. Those precious times established a foundation for us to build a mother/daughter relationship.

"Doug likes to call it 'slumber party talk' where the defenses of the day cease, the emotional and physical energy drop, and the talk flows like water downstream. I heard Mom speak of her dreams, her disappointments, her doubts, and her daily life. We talked like friends talk—real, open, attentive, forgiving. Every now and then I find myself, twenty-five years later and three kids deep into my own motherhood, wishing I could just sit in the late night stillness of my parent's living room and talk with my mom. I'm honored to say I get along with my mom and we are friends. I am grateful for our relationship."

What does it mean to have a good relationship with your child? One phrase from young people says it all:

We get along.

What does it mean to have a poor or non-existent relationship with your child? Another simple statement summarizes what kids told us:

We don't get along.

From the Southwest to the Northwest to the Midwest, throughout the country and across the socio-economic groupings, we found kids talking about a relationship with mom in terms of either getting along with her or not. Over 17 percent of the young people we sought out used the specific phrase "get along" to define their relationship with their mom.

Twelve-year-old Phillip lands on the positive side. He told us:

My relationship with my mom is a ten. We get along very well.

One fifteen-year-old male chose to remain anonymous. He told us:

We don't get along at all, even if we try. She's not the kind of person I can talk to and tell her what's going on!

We already noted that the heart of a mother/child relationship is communication between them. If communication is the heart, "getting along" is the vital sign: the heart rate and blood pressure of the relationship.

Kids treat relationships as though they and those around them are traveling somewhere. If you connect with your child, you go with him or her on that trip. If you don't communicate, you don't get along and you don't travel together through life.

What does it mean to get along? For many young people, getting along means being friends. This chapter offers the third Cheer of the Heart: We get along. If a subtitle was used, the child might be saying, We are friends.

Mom, to rate high in a relationship you know you must communicate at the highest level. If your child says, I can tell my mom anything, you will also hear your child say, *We get along.* If you get along with your child, consider yourself a friend. One out of ten kids we talked to view their mom as a friend. One out of twenty gave their mom a ten on the rating scale. Do you get the picture? Kids don't exclude us old folks from the friendship scale!

First, let's get a grasp on what kids are looking for in friendship. Then we can ask, "What's a mother to do?"

WHAT KIDS LOOK FOR IN A FRIEND

Kamy, a nineteen-year-old young woman gives divine credit to her relationship with her mom. Kamy says:

The Lord has really opened the doors to allowing us not only to have a relationship but also a friendship. We have the qualities of a friendship between us.

Sixteen-year-old Laurie described the different roles her mom plays in her life, including the spiritual dynamic. She stated:

I can tell my mother everything; she listens and gives good advice. She is my guider, protector, friend, and spiritual adviser.

You might think of friendship with your child as a continual investment in maintaining your most important life treasure, one you carried around in hiding for roughly nine months before you could see the precious gift.

What can you do to keep things moving along? First you must find the qualities of a friendship and live them out with your child. We assembled a small group of pediatric professionals, people who know what a child needs in a relationship to keep things moving along and growing. Our panel of experts has a few things in common. First, they are all in their adolescence. Second, they get along with their moms—contrary to popular opinion about teenagers and their parents today.

Meet our panelists:

Olivia, age seventeen

Valerie, age thirteen

Nicole, age twelve

Megan, age fourteen

Eric, age thirteen

Tiara, age fourteen

Corrina, age seventeen

Here's what they said about the friendships with their moms:

Olivia says:

My mom is a trusted friend to me. We respect one another. Thank you for working so hard for me and for being so supportive.

I agree, says Valerie, *we're best friends. I know my mom wants the best for me.*

What can a mom and her child do to make the relationship special?

Nicole states:

Even though I'm only twelve, we do everything together. We're like best friends.

Then Megan pipes in:

I appreciate all the time my mom gives up to make my life special.

Hey, don't let the guys be left out. Eric, any comment?

Sure! My mom and I get along well. We share a lot with each other; we do a lot together.

Not bad for someone who is not only younger, but also a different gender.

Finally Tiara speaks up:

I can relate to all of these kids. My mom and I talk and do stuff and are friends.

Corrina, any final comments?

Sure, my mom is one of my best friends and she is always there for me. She is supportive of me no matter what.

To sum it all up:

- Friends support each other.
- Friends want the best for their friends.
- Friends do stuff and spend time together.
- Friends talk.
- Friends are always there for each other.

We have listed some general qualities we consider to exist between friends. Your best bet is to ask your child for his or her definition of a friendship. You may want to write your own top-ten list of friendship qualities and then ask your child to do the same. Compare the list to see how close you two are in defining your needs. Once you get the list, you've got some practical and tangible ways to get along better with your child.

WHAT'S A MOTHER TO DO?

With the qualities and quotes from kids in mind, we offer some words of encouragement to help you build your relationship with your child—be it a budding or bumbling friendship. Here are three ways to help you get along with your child:

- Befriend your child.
- Find a friend for yourself.
- Be a mother to your child.

Befriend Your Child

Treat your child like you would treat a friend, or better yet, like you want to be treated. To befriend denotes initiative on mom's part. Mom, you birthed the child. The greater responsibility lies on you as the birth mother, the adult and caretaker in the relationship. The responsibility may shift as your child grows older into adulthood, but if your child is still under age twenty, you lead the dance. Here are a few practical suggestions from our panel for you to instigate a friendship: "Do stuff," "Be honest," and "Share interests."

Do stuff. In the words of your child, "Just do stuff." Do means act—go, leave, move, travel. To befriend a child is to simply do stuff. The *type* of stuff will vary from kid to kid. One young person told us,

I always go places with my mom. I'm not afraid to be seen with her because we are so close. It's like she's one of my friends because we do a lot together.

Brenna, fifteen years old

For Brenna, what she and her mom do is not important. In Chapter 2, we encouraged you to date your child one-on-one. The same action step applies here. You can even broaden the "date" to include other people and do things in groups.

Before you pass out, Mom, watch your child with her friends. What they do is seldom spectacular or expensive. They just do stuff.

We believe an incredible challenge for most moms is finding the time and energy to do more with their children when life is already so busy. Mom, first make a commitment to do, in keeping with the time and energy you can afford. Next, figure out what stuff your kid wants to do with you. In Chapter 8 we'll give you some creative ideas.

What if you don't spend time doing stuff with your child? Listen to one young girl named Marieanne:

Our relationship is a five. We get along, but sometimes we fight. We don't usually spend much time together.

Marieanne is two years older than Brenna. We wonder what would have happened if Marieanne's mom had started doing stuff with her daughter when she was Brenna's age. Would the relationship rate higher than a five? We think so.

Once you're doing, you're ready to start being.

Be honest. Friendship is like pizza, most people love it, but they have their personal preference for what they want on it. If we dropped by your house one night around 5:17 p.m. (FST) with a pizza in hand as a gift to your family, our guess is you would rise up and call us blessed. But how would you feel about pizza with toppings of anchovies, onions, peanut butter, and lima beans? No matter how hard we tried, we may have offered you something you didn't want.

Friendships are subjective. What one person considers friendly, another considers invasive. Mom, you and your child need to reach a level of shared honesty before you can become friends. If you don't know what your child likes, and you keep forcing lima beans and anchovies, you could push your child away as quickly as you can say Domino's Pizza.

Honesty helps build true friendships and keeps them true. Listen to one young person speak of how well she gets along with her mom:

My mom and I get along well. I'm always honest with her. If I have a problem I go straight to my mom.

Ironically, this young girl's name is Destiney. Mom, if you want your effort of befriending your child to leave a lasting destiny, be honest with yourself and your child. Another young person feels the same openness in her relationship with her mom. They always get along because . . .

We know everything about each other.
Why? Her mom is the color white, because she is . . .
pure, clean, and always tells the truth.
Nicole, thirteen years old

One sixteen-year-old chose not to tell us his name, but his candidness does not bother us. He said:

My mom and I are best friends. We fight sometimes but I guess no relationship is perfect. I really feel like I can tell her anything.

Three cheers for moms who can fight sometimes with their kids and still get along like best friends. Kim, who is fifteen years old, let us know it is not as easy for her to share all with her mom. She says:

I'm not always open with my mom but we get along really well besides.

Mom, remember two things. Your child wants your presence not your perfection. Secondly, it is your child's choice (possibly influenced by your child's action) that determines how honest he or she will be. In other words, you have your intuition and your influence to open the heart of your child, but you can't make it happen. You can't force honesty, but you can give it.

Share interests. Just mention that you are from the same hometown, college, or sorority to a complete stranger who shares that experience and you feel as though you just found a lost cousin. For men, friendships are often made on the ball field or the battlefield. That's a key reason for the proliferation of so many adult sports leagues in our society. Men need a place to find commonality. Men would be lost if life was nothing more than dinner and a movie. Men need to *do*.

Of course, a dinner date may be the ultimate apex of a male/female relationship. At dinner, both genders can do what they love to do: Women can share the company and conversation of another individual with whom they have an interest; men can eat. It's a win/win for both genders.

"Common Bond" is a simple icebreaker we use at conferences and retreats to help people get to know each other in a short amount of time. The participants are asked to pair up with someone they don't know. They are then given a few minutes to find things they have in common.

One of the most amazing bonds we've seen was between two men who realized they not only lived in the same town many years prior, they had both dated and were engaged to the same woman at different times—a young lady neither ended up marrying. They became fast friends. Try playing the game some time in a group of people. You will be amazed at how many links people find with complete strangers.

To befriend your child is to find "common ground." The strength not only enables you to get along better, it helps to oppose the communication block of uncommonality we mentioned in Chapter 5. Mom, you can take the simple game of "Common Bond" and play it with your child. Find thirty things you have in common. They may include stuff you can do together. They may be fears you have never shared before such as: "I'm afraid of very high heights."

Another way to find shared interests is to take a personality inventory—a tool to help people better understand why they act the way they do. We suggest the Taylor-Johnson or Myers-Briggs personality inventory. (See Appendix B for suggestions on where you may obtain these materials.) Personality tests may also unveil some points of conflict you have with your child (or spouse) that you could not understand. Take precautions: the tests are not to be used as a means to pigeon-hole people or to limit their ability to grow as a person.

One thirteen-year-old told us a strength to her relationship with her mom was their shared personality:

We have the same personality, so we get along pretty good.

A final area of shared interest is brought to light by a seventeen year old named Rob. He shared the strength of his relationship with his mom with us by stating:

We get along very well and we pray together.

Much like Kamy and Laurie, two young women who helped us begin this chapter, Rob places his faith at the center of his relationship with his mom. You may have heard the phrase, "The family that prays together, stays together." We can point to three young people who concur with this idiom. Praying together puts what is most important in your life at the center of your relationship. While you are there before God, ask for the ability to be friends. Remember, He is the one who exemplified and coined the phrase, "Greater love has no one than this, than to lay down one's life for his friends."[1]

Before you know it, you too may be on the receiving end of a statement like this:

My mom is one of my closest friends.
Sheri, fifteen years old

Befriend your child, then find a friend for yourself.

Find a Friend for Yourself

We want to be very clear on this next point. Being a friend and looking for a friend are different. When you befriend, you work from your strength and your love to build into someone else. When you seek a friend, you search for a relationship from both your strengths and your weaknesses, your resources and your needs. Mom, we exhort you to befriend your child but we encourage you to find other relationships.

If you are ready, we want to ask you to consider a few important questions:

1. What do you need personally from your relationship with your child?
2. What needs of your own are not being met by your husband? What drives you to your child to have these needs met?

Too many moms go to their kids to meet needs that a child is not able to provide. To summarize the above two questions: When it comes to a close friend, with whom do you share your heart?

If you are quick to answer, "I don't have any free time for a deep friendship," your life is out of balance. You will place expectations on your children they won't be able to deliver.

The second question deals with your marriage. Many women marry their best friend, who in turn becomes a man who is only the father of their children. If a wife moves away from seeing her husband as a friend and begins to see him merely as a paternal caretaker, she is treading on dangerous ground.

To keep your marriage fresh and healthy, you have got to keep your spouse as your friend. If he has become only your husband (your marriage mate) or the father of your children, which is even farther removed, an important part of your life will be vacant. Women who live with a man who is only the father of their children often move from being the mother of their children to the friend of their children. And some women find a friend in another man (who may likely be married to a woman who is the mother of his children) and leave their children in a world of hurt, distrust, and pain. The kids then seek out a family relationship with their peers through gangs and sexual promiscuity.

Mom, if you're empty you can't be a friend. No relationship with a child, no matter how well you get along, can replace what you need from your spouse.

We offer special encouragement to single moms who may carry guilt from the divorce. This mom may neglect her own needs as a sacrifice to redeem the broken family. To care for a child and recover from the pain of the past, these single moms desperately need a friend.

Once again we turn to young people to gain some insight from their perspective.

Sixteen-year-old Shaun says:

Mom, if I could say anything I would tell you, do something for yourself.

Mom, do something for yourself. Find a friend. You'll be a stronger mom in the process.

Be a Mom

Mom, take a look in the mirror. Unless you resemble someone your child's age, don't act like one. Sure, you can befriend your child, but your child needs other friends just like you do. Your task is to clarify what it means to be a mom who befriends her child without being her child's friend. Listen to a couple of young people explain their needs in a mom:

> *To try to be a mom and not a best friend.*
> Mandy, fifteen years old

> *We are like friends, but not like friends at school.*
> Bill, thirteen years old

Mandy is looking for a mom, not a best friend. She can find one of those in a league of her own. Would she turn down a mom who treats her as mom would like to be treated? Most likely not. But she does not want a mom to share a secret part of her that she does not think is fit for mothers.

Bill considers his mother a friend, but she is different from his friends at school. At age thirteen, Bill may or may not articulate the difference between a maternal home friend and an external school friend, but he does know there is a difference.

In the Webster family, we find ourselves saying to our daughters as they interact with their siblings, "Remember, you are not the mother. Your job is to be the sister. Let Mom be Mom, and Dad be Dad."

It's time to look yourself in the mirror and say, "Remember, you are not the sibling or the neighborhood friend. You are mom. Now, act out your part."

A manager's goal is not to be popular, but to be effective. Not every decision made by the manager is going to be received with shouts of joy from the employees.

Mom, sorry to say, your job is no different. Your purpose as a mom is not to develop a fan club, but to raise responsible children. Mothers are not celebrities in the home, they are more like stage managers. Without them, the show would never go on, but the glory does not arrive until the end of the production. If you are looking to be highly esteemed for every effort, get out of the mothering business. Motherhood is not a volunteer position; it is only paid like it is.

Mom, to avoid some of the common battles, first, establish clear boundaries. If the boundaries are not clear, land can be claimed with a "nine-tenths" possession mentality. For example, if curfew is: "Don't come home late," the word late is all too relative. Even if the curfew is definite—11:00 p.m.—and the consequences equal "You're going to get grounded, mister," a battle may still arise the next morning. Your version of "grounded" may be quite different from your son's. He will likely battle for a lesser sentencing if he knows he can wear you down with the war. Better to say, "Being late—meaning any minute past 11:00 p.m.—equals a day of grounding from your radio, the television, and the phone. Every ten minutes late earns you another day." Your child may find a few more loopholes, but the majority of the weapons have been removed because the guidelines are very clear. When you are clear, it is easier to say, "No discussion necessary, I was very clear."

Here are a few contrasts between a friend and a mom:

- Friends have persuasion. Moms have power.
- Friends encourage. Moms exhort.
- A friend says, "You should." A mom says, "You will."
- A friend says, "Oh well, hopefully next time." A mom says, "You cannot afford a next time."

Mom, you are walking a high tightrope, minus the net. Don't take the task lightly. It cannot be mastered in a moment or manipulated in a minute.

Listen to what fourteen-year-old Katie has to say about her mom:

It's hard for me to open up to her like I could when I was little. It seems ever since I entered high school she is the parent, the one making the rules, and not my friend.

We can read what Katie said, but what she means has a sting. Mom hears:

You're not the nice mom you use to be.
You are a parent and you use to be my friend.
You care more about rules than you care about me.
Ever since I entered high school, you don't trust me.

Kids know how to send zingers right through mom's bulletproof vest to penetrate the heart. When a child shoots razor-tipped verbiage toward mom, mom begins to question her ability as a nurturing parent. The "ouch factor" is most effective with a woman suffering from poor self-care and low self-esteem. When a mom is more concerned about how much she is liked than how effective she is in raising a child, the woman is vulnerable to attack.

Mom, you've got to hold your course or you will lose ground quickly. It may take years before you see the positive reward of your work, but it will pay off. Teri's mom had to wait many years before she heard that blessing she no doubt longed to hear. Her daughter tells us that the relationship is a ten because . . .

She loves me and was never afraid to discipline me in a loving manner. She encourages me without pushing, and she has always been there for me. She's more than my mother; she's my best friend!

Teri's mom was never afraid to act in the best long-term interest of her child, in spite of the inevitable short-term barriers and battles. One young girl of thirteen even saw the value of mom being a mom. She told us:

My relationship with my mom is a ten. Why? Because she provides me with everything and punishes me when I need it.

Many of us see the power in authority even if we dislike its punch. Believe it or not, even kids value guidelines.

We are calling moms to a lost art. It is called discipline. One English man was noted as saying, "It is delightful to see how well parents in America *obey their children.*" What a reversal!

Let's break the cycle in today's culture. Mom, be a mother. You may find your child feeling the same way this sixteen-year-old does:

My mom is like the color pink—very feminine and ladylike. She's raised me like that, too. It's very cool because she is old-fashioned but at the same time she's strong.

Mom can be feminine and friendly and strong to boot—old fashioned but cool!

In two previous chapters we let Ciara grant us the wisdom of babes to create a focus for the role of mom. Her insights were:

1. Stay close.
2. Share conflicts.
3. Send cheers.

We want to add a fourth responsibility to mom's job description:

4. Stay in charge.

You can give your child a promotion or grant him or her a raise, but just don't give up the title of mom.

A funny thing may happen if you strive to befriend your child, find a friend for yourself, and be a mother to your child. You may succeed in all three. If so, your child will be fortunate to share Marvin and Anjee's sentiments:

She is a mom and a friend at the same time.

Marvin, eighteen years old

I can tell her anything and we not only have a mother/daughter relationship, but also a friendship.

Anjee, sixteen years old

WHAT IF MY CHILD DOESN'T WANT TO SPEND TIME WITH ME?

Some moms and dads have asked us, "What if my child doesn't want to spend time with me?" He or she may not want to for a variety of reasons, including the fact that the child may simply be too busy. One seventeen-year-old girl said:

Mom, sometimes I know you think that I'm too busy for you, but I want you to know that I'll always need you no matter what.

If you offer the gift of your time and your child refuses, you can't force them, especially for kids age seventeen and older. This doesn't mean that you can't pass on an edict that there *will* be family times and the kids *will* attend. You are still mom. But if the event is voluntary and your child doesn't want what you offer, let it go. Be honest with your disappointment. Communicate the value you place on your time together. And if possible, let your child know the offer stands and can be redeemed when he or she is ready.

WHAT IF I DON'T WANT TO SPEND TIME WITH MY CHILD?

We wish there were wise ways and witty words to make

this feeling go away, but there is no easy way out. A breath of fresh air blows through motherdom when you hear a transparent mom say:

Right now, I love my child, but I really don't like my child.

Most moms are afraid to go public with such a notion (again, the ouch factor: being perceived as uncaring), but it is probably more common than many believe. What do you do? Choose to love your child and be with your child. You do stuff with your child anyway. Since when is committed love driven by passion and pleasure? That ended somewhere between "I do" and "I'm pregnant." Now it is time for adults to love like adults, in spite of the discomfort. Hang in there, Mom, you're not alone and this too shall pass. Your heart will follow your head.

WHAT IF I DON'T GET ALONG AND MY BEFRIENDING HAS BACKFIRED?

What if your household reflects the statements of a twelve-year-old named Scott?

My mom and I fight a lot. We don't get along very well. Sometimes we do.

The opposite of getting along with mom is arguing with mom. We wish you could have looked over our shoulders as we poured through the responses from kids. We saw a very distinct pattern of the words *argue* and *fight* as we descended in the ratings. Kids at a ten state how well they get along with mom because they are friends. Level nine relationships show slight signs of fights or disagreements—they were to be expected—but they still get along fabulously with mother. Around the rating of eight, we began to see more kids refer to the amount of fighting, arguing, or yelling with their moms.

Even worse, kids with ratings three and under seldom or never get along with their moms. They spend most of their time arguing.

Mom, here is a simple way to determine the rating of your relationship with your child. How loud is your home? The more you and your child raise your voices in disagreement, the farther the rating will drop.

Do relationships rated ten signal no family arguments? Not if those families are human. Not all fights are bad. However, when you or your child screams, the relationship runs a risk of plummeting because you come desperately close to a relational cardiac arrest due to a blocked heart. The next chapter deals with the third tear of the heart: *Quit yelling and chill out!*

> *Dear Mom,*
>
> *Thanks for always being there for me. We get along so well and you're like a best friend to me. I enjoy the time we spend together, and I know we will always be close.*
>
> *Love,*
> *Your child*

Chapter 7

> *Dear Mom,*
>
> *Quit yelling and chill out!*
>
> *Love,*
> *Your child*

QUIT YELLING AND
CHILL OUT!

I never know when she is going to be mad at me.
Todd, fourteen years old

Mom, you are like the color red. When you get mad, you get really mad. It is really hard to talk to you.
Female, thirteen years old

Mom, you are the color red because you're always mad. Our relationship is a two because we always fight. I want to tell you to shut up.
Jeff, thirteen years old

Hurricane Marilyn hit the U.S. Virgin Islands in September of 1995 with incredible force. It was an awesome and frightful sight to see on TV large sailboats cast on their sides in the middle of the street, far from shore. People on the island—many of them travelers from foreign countries—were terrified by the sheer force of nature as the wind and water literally picked up vessels and cast them on high, like a child playing with a boat in the bathtub. A few of the people interviewed by newscasters spoke of their first time experience in a hurricane.

One young couple looked like they were midway through their honeymoon. They clung to each other as they recanted facing the hurricane from the window in their oceanfront hotel room. Imagine their response when they got back to Iowa and someone asked, "How was your honeymoon?"

"Well, you know us. We really shook the place up!"

Few of us have to think hard to remember Hurricane Marilyn's older brother, Andrew, which left a swath of destruction as it blew its way through Florida not many years ago. When a hurricane hits, no one can predict its severity. There is always a sense of "Hold on and pray!"

Robin does not want to imagine what a hurricane and possible tidal wave is like to experience. *The Long Journey Home: The Adventures of Yellow Dog* is one of our kids' favorite movies. Robin could not watch the scene when the large wave hits the boat and sends the boy and his dog into the sea. The mere thought gives her nightmares. (*The Poseidon Adventure* was never a two-thumbs up movie for her.)

Yet few of us born and raised in Southern California know what it is to encounter a hurricane. We Southern Californians have earthquakes, however. They hit unexpectedly, last indefinitely, and return without warning with sometimes up to thousands of aftershocks in the same area. After a few biggies, one only needs to feel a jolt or roll of the ground and his fear meter hits the top. The last major earthquake was centered in Northridge near Los Angeles during a time when we were separated from our children.

We were enjoying a wonderful weekend in Lake Arrowhead with two other couples. As you know, getting time away with dear friends—minus children—is next to impossible. We were savoring every moment—until the earth moved. The early morning shaker awakened us, casting us into each other's arms until the movement stopped. Then we stumbled out to the common area of the cabin where other pajama-covered, sleepy-eyed adults were standing and staring at one another in complete shock.

A few thoughts pass ever so quickly through your mind in the midst of an earthquake: *How long will this go on? Will it get worse?*

Another earthquake hit two years prior when Robin was nearly full term with her third pregnancy. A fast jump to her feet and a dart across a moving house was almost enough to bring our son into the world right in the living room. One immediate concern pushed all other thoughts aside: *The kids! Get the kids!* A quick phone call home let us know our area was shaken but not broken.

That settled, two new questions arose: How bad was the quake? And where was it centered?

Not much later, Robin returned upstairs to awaken Doug with the tearful proclamation, "Doug, it's really bad. They are showing clips on TV." Hundreds died and thousands were left homeless for many days on end. Parks in the Northridge area became makeshift camp grounds, filled with people who feared their roofs might collapse on them if they returned home.

Mom, this sounds like a lesson on seismology or weather patterns, but we are here to talk about another type of disaster—family disasters. They are all too common and much more readily encountered than hurricanes, earthquakes, and tornados.

Some kids in families today want to report a hurricane in their home. The question "What color best describes your mom?" revealed the emotional side of mother/child relationships. Some want to ring a loud alarm with a powerful, emotional message for mom:

Mom, quit yelling and chill out!

Thirteen-year-old Ryan was one to ring the bell. He said, *My mom is the color blue like the ocean. Sometimes she can be calm and loving and make me feel great. Other times, things she says crumble my heart like a big wave coming at me, throwing me down.*

Ryan speaks like that master of the seas who guided the Queen Elizabeth II through the ninety-five foot wave. Anyone who thinks, "How bad can a mad mom be?" has never been around an infuriated mother on a stormy day. From what we hear from the kids, they are as serious as a hurricane. Their S.O.S call is no joking matter.

As the young people have helped us learn, there are four levels of communication between a mother and her child:

- I can tell you anything.
- I can tell you almost anything.
- I can't tell you everything.
- I can't tell you anything.

The Quit yelling and chill out! message is often near the

bottom in good communication. It is a last-ditch effort from a child saying:

I can't take it anymore. Your anger has blocked me completely away from you. Not only do we not have much of a relationship, I cannot get anything across to you. My only way to communicate with you is to yell like you do.

How serious is this cry of a child's heart? Listen close, Mom, for we have seen a debilitating impact on many families. *Quit yelling and chill out* may be the last communique before the child reaches the uncharted, deserted island of the message, *I can live without you*. Sad to say for too many children, both young and adult, the trip in the Chill Hurricane to the Without You Island is a short voyage.

If you have ever heard the statement, *Mom, quit yelling and chill out!* drop everything and go for higher ground. The statement is a declaration of the final block to the heart between a mother and her child: the block of anger, which we mentioned in Chapter 5. We heard such strong comments from the young people, we believe it is necessary for moms to get the report as clearly and directly as we can relay it.

If you are fortunate to have never experienced such a statement firsthand, congratulations! But you probably do not have to look far down your street or across your extended family to find remnants of a hurricane. You may pick up some lifesaving skills you can pass on to a friend, neighbor, or family member. If you know someone who will benefit from understanding the "Hurricane Mom" message, they don't have a great deal of time to waste. Likely, there is already damage done.

In this chapter we will focus on the power and presence of anger in the family. Then, with an eye for a brighter, clearer tomorrow, we ask the question again, "What's a mother to do?" Practical encouragement is offered as a lifeline of hope for a sinking mom.

First, let's look at the powerful pull of pain.

THE POWER OF PAIN

A commercial jingle for a pain reliever borrows from a famous song: "I haven't got time for the pain." Few of us go looking for pain. But, oh how easily it finds us! Like a military officer, General Pain has a way of commanding our attention, forcing us to stand up and salute, or drop down and beg.

Pain can mean hurting emotions, hurting bodies, hurting relationships, hurting finances. But pain is only a symptom of something deeper.

We believe kids are saying *Mom, quit yelling and chill out!* because of pain. We hear kids point to two sore spots. First, their own pain, and secondly, their mom's pain.

The Child's Pain

Sixteen-year-old Jay gave his relationship with his mom a meager four. You may recall this is lower than the average number from kids who. say, *I can't say anything to my mom.* Jay said:

We love each other, but I don't like talking to her. I don't tell her anything. She doesn't know me and doesn't trust me. If I could tell my mom anything, I would say, "The things you yell at me for are not worth ruining my day. It just makes me want to do them."

Jay's mom is a source of pain. Mom, wait and listen before you argue that the son may be a louse of a kid. Think about what's happening here. If mom's goal is to motivate her son to get him to do something he is not doing, it is obviously not working.

Some kids go as far as shutting mom off when she hits a certain volume level. If the child is older, or too scarred from previous emotional scalding, the child will muster up the courage to say, "Mom, chill it!" Cool off, drop the temp, turn down the heat. This kid is trying to communiate, "You are not giving me life. You are sucking it away."

If the child is not speaking about his pain from his mom, he may be referring to the pain he has caused for himself. Another sixteen-year-old young man named Jesse takes more of the failure on his own shoulders. He told us:

Whatever I've done in the past I always regret.

Here we find a kid in pain from what he has done, not what mom has done. It is interesting to learn the color Jesse painted his mother:

My mom is like the color white for goodness and purity. My mother has taught me to be good in a world that's full of darkness. I love my mom and I'm very thankful for having her.

Jesse is aware of right and wrong, good and evil, darkness and light. He owes these insights to his mother's teaching and modeling. Not all young people make their confession to their moms so willingly.

Some kids take their pain from personal experience and dump it on mom. Who is to blame for the shipwreck? It may be due to the hurricane, but it also may be the result of an inexperienced crew or a faulty vessel. Even in the calmest seas, a careless sailor can lead a vessel and crew to destruction by the actions he takes. Some pain in the home is the direct result of a child's actions and mom ends up with the blame.

Then again, some pain in the family comes from the nature of mother and it rains down on the children.

Mom's Pain

Good ol' wisdom told us earlier: "If mamma ain't happy, ain't nobody happy."

Listen to the second verse of the same imaginary song, "If mamma is in pain, the whole family is in a world of hurt."

If pain is the symptom, not the cause, where does mom's pain come from? Again, many places push the pain. We draw your attention to three key areas:

- Pain of the past (family upbringing and former romantic relationships)
- Pain of the present (marriage and the kids)
- Physical pain (mom's health)

The pain of mom's past. A thirteen-year-old female could

have written an entire book when we asked her about her mom. Listen as she pours out her heart. She states:

My mom is like the color dark blue, and our relationship is a six on the scale. Lately, we are more like sisters. Ever since the divorce, we fight a lot. I think I have a good understanding of her pain. I am not sure the understanding is returned by her. It takes two to make it work.

Let's look at the meaning behind what she says:

We are more like sisters.	The roles have changed.
Ever since the divorce . . .	Mom's past is painful.
We fight a lot.	The pain is present.
Understanding is not returned.	The channel is blocked.
It takes two to make it work.	Mom has given up.

She continues:

I have a right to reasons. I have opinions and parents are not always right. Kids have certain rights.

Typically when people need to claim their rights, they feel they have been wronged in some way.

Then she adds this brain twister:

I know you believe what you think I said, but I am not sure you realize what you heard is not what I meant.

In other words, mom doesn't get it. Worse yet, she thinks she does! This young girl desperately wants to communicate with her mom at a higher level, but she may soon find her only cry to be, Mom, quit yelling and chill out! She may even lack the energy to speak so boldly. Then she will disappear. We call it running away. The child concludes, *I can live without you.*

Mom, how has your past influenced your present relationship with your child? Is there unfinished business from a previous marriage or relationship? Or are you like many woman attempting to sort out their role as a mother with the confusing and complex experiences from their own past with their parents? Do you come up empty when you look for a role model of a healthy mother/child relationship? One woman recently told us, "I never heard my parents say, 'I love you' or 'I am sorry.' Never."

Mom, your kids pay the price. If Hurricane Mom keeps dashing the family against the rocks, they will cry out, "No more!" Some moms don't have to look back to find pain, they can look around and spot the pain in the present.

The pain of mom's present. If the pain of the past is a walk through the scrapbook of memories, the pain of the present is a brave look in the mirror . . . or across the table . . . or next to you in bed . . . or down the hall. Let's take a look at two possible places of pain: marriage and children.

Marriage can cause a great deal of pain for a mom. And if mom's in pain, kids can spot it, sometimes even more clearly than mom. Fifteen-year-old Melissa said:

I think she and dad should get counseling, and if that doesn't work, get divorced.

Although we don't recommend what may be a hasty or naive diagnosis and prescription, if your marriage is in pain, do something about it. We value the presence of marriage as the vehicle God has designed, ordained, and used to bring people into the world and teach them the ways of life and love. We also believe the most effective way to raise balanced, healthy kids who make a positive difference in our society is for the father to love the mother in a lifelong commitment of marriage.

Mom, invest in your marriage. The work is taxing but the alternative is costly. Divorce is a death that does not pass away although people do find healing and recovery. We have not met a kid who has said, "My folks got a divorce and it's great. It's so good, I wish they would have been divorced before they ever got married."

If your marriage is not a source of pain, the by-product of the relationship—your kids—may be the sore spot. Raising children is the most difficult undertaking many of us will ever encounter. Think about it. If it was so easy and enjoyable, we would have lots of kids. Yet the average family in the United States has more televisions than kids. Where do we spend our free time? Sad to say, most pick the tube over the child.

Our society has become more computer friendly than child friendly. We don't think twice about jumping on the Internet to enjoy a chat with a complete stranger. Mom, you may not even have to go outside to find your challenge. It may be waiting for you down the hall in the likes of a child who resembles you and carries your genes. Even some kids realize how tough it is to raise them. Listen to what these two have to say:

I know I'm hard to handle . . . you're doing a great job.
Tiffany, thirteen years old

I'm a teenager. . . . fights happen.
Anonymous

Young people know all about the challenge of raising teenagers. It's no picnic. Childhood is a time of powerful emotional, physical, mental, and social changes. Few changes happen gradually, many happen constantly, and the fun changes happen overnight. Our dear friends who have encountered these changes tell us, "It's so interesting to watch our kids go into the bathroom in the morning. We wait with expectation to see who is going to come out. We've seen real monsters come out of the bathroom and we always wonder, 'What did they see in there to cause this?' We'll never know."

Parenting really has two romantic eras, followed by two periods of adolescence. Generally speaking, the first romantic era occurs from birth through age three. (Mind you, this era may not coincide with the romantic era in the marriage!) The first pass at adolescence, what we call "premature adolescence," occurs around age two and lasts anywhere from a few months to two years in an average family. It is affectionately known as "the terrible-twos." Mom, if you treat your toddler like an adolescent in training, you will have a whole new perspective on the challenge. Instead of asking for the car keys, toddlers just throw them in the toilet, which has virtually the same result.

The second romantic era begins somewhere around age

four and lasts to the late grade school years. It is more elongated and less acute than the first romantic era. One passage of this era occurs at age five or six when the child goes to kindergarten. Mom is pained at first, but she begins to find moments of personal peace, including a possible return of her own choice of activity or less guilt while away at work. Doug likes to say, "That's why we pay taxes, to send our kids to school and regain some sanity."

The second and most pronounced adolescent era comes as anticipated, but it is funny how it sneaks up on so many unsuspecting parents. We believe some moms and dads are in a parental trance of romantic complacency, allowing themselves to be caught off guard when puberty attacks. Mom and dad are thinking, "This parental thing is working nicely. The kids have the family system down. They are pretty much maintenance free. They understand the rules. We have more status than their peers. They lack the finances, the physical stature, the street savvy, or the hormones to consider any overthrow of authority. Ah, the good life of the family! Isn't it almost romantic?"

Then one morning that child innocently walks into the bathroom and disappears. The twelve-year-old child is gone, abducted by the powers of puberty. As much as mom and dad have enjoyed seven years of feasting, they have just entered seven years of family famine—the last and most intense years of passage.

Surprise, Mom, you have a newfound source of pain in your life! Your child turned teenager. As that anonymous teen said, "I'm a teenager. Fights happen." What did you expect, Mom, a walk in the park on a moonlit night with someone you love? The romance is gone. The renaissance is over. Welcome to the Dark Ages.

Hurting marriages and changing children are two areas that can be a source of pain for moms. A third possible bleeder is a combination of the these two areas. One young person told us:

I get along better with dad.

Thanks, Mom says to herself. The comparison of the relationship a child has with her dad can be a powerful leverage tool for the savvy young person. Add the child's manipulations to a hurting marriage between mom and her husband, and presto, you've got yourself instant combustion that cranks up the family anger. Kids learn quickly how to maneuver feelings and responsibilities around the house to create a nicely woven web of emotions. Moms can find themselves trapped in pain from their kids via their husbands.

When researching *Dear Dad*, Doug discovered a high level of anger between young people and their fathers. One in six kids used the words anger, angry, or *mad* to describe their dads. We are raising a generation of enraged kids because they live with mad dads. A father's anger is one of the three barriers to a relationship with his child (along with absence and authority). And mom may find herself trying to be a cool breeze to shade the heat of dad's blistering sun. When mom tries too hard, she may run into her own high pressure system.

People such as husbands, significant others, ex-husbands, or the offspring can be very effective at hitting a sore spot in mom. They represent the most significant sources of pain, but sad to say, not the only places of hurt. Add in-laws, parents, neighbors, business associates, subordinates or bosses, and you have a bus load of potential pain.

Another person may be the primary source of your pain: you.

Pain of the Physical Body

You know the challenge of keeping your body in good health after a tiny human being charged through a very small area with the force of a runaway train. A mom in physical pain trying to face the ordinary demands of motherhood with a body that won't follow suit can be a woman in double pain. Mom, how is your health? Do you sleep well at night? When was the last time you had a good stretch of rest, and not just a good night's sleep.

Or how long has it been since you have maintained a consistent exercise program? (We are not talking about the "gotta lose weight and be a cover girl" kind of push.) Maybe a general physical from a doctor is your first step when your kids want to check out because of your anger.

Throw in personal and physical anguish, and you have a mom who only has to look in the mirror to find the person behind her pain.

And we must not forget those endless inanimate objects. Here are just a few of those pain pushers in a typical mom's life:

Traffic

Lines at stores

Dual careers: home and work

Work deadlines

Soccer practice

Car pool

Homework management

Dinner

Checkbooks

Credit card payments

Filling the car with gas

Rotting food in the refrigerator

Need we go on? It's no wonder some moms are screaming mad and their kids are saying, *Quit yelling and chill out!* You can understand why a girl like Charissa says to her mom:

Mom, you need to calm down a little bit.

And a sixteen-year-old said:

My mom is the color red. She freaks out a lot. Just chill out!

Mom, a solid way to find your pain is too look around at the *who* or *what* is causing the hurt. Once you've identified the fuel behind the fire, it is easier to deal with the burn of the flame.

THE POWER OF ANGER

The late Richard Nixon offered a powerful piece of reality

in his book, *1999*. He wrote: "We live in a world with nuclear weapons. Since that fact is not going to change, we must learn to live with the bomb."[1]

We were struck by that statement's relevance to the nuclear family today. Anger is present and we must learn to live with it. Anger can be a weapon launched as an attack on a child like a smart bomb fired over enemy lines. It can create a family meltdown.

Anger is not only powerful in a destructive force, anger is a powerful revelation. Since anger is not primary, but a response to something else, anger is also a link to the heart of the mad person. Mom, when you identify someone's anger, you are close to his or her soul.

If someone is angry it may be because you stepped on their toes. The closer your are, the more likely you will hear the "Ouch!" So in a peculiar way, anger can be a very strong link to intimacy if handled correctly. When you get close you become intimate, or "in-to-a-mate." Intimacy is far beyond sex. Intimacy is sharing what's most important, most dear, and most treasured to you. Look at the power of anger this way, Mom: conflict is an exciting way to reveal concerns, develop character, practice communication, and extend compassion.

M. Scott Peck offers his experience as both a medical doctor and a therapist in his book, *A World Waiting to Be Born*. He helps us realize that pain is not always bad. A healthy life is not a life without pain. One of the worst diseases imaginable is leprosy because it creates a situation of painlessness, leaving its victims with destroyed nerves, or pain-free bodies. A leper will get burned if he is too close to a flame because he may not notice the damage being done to his body. When you and I feel the heat of the flame, we move away for fear of getting burned. The pain protects us from worse damage. Peck writes:

We need to experience pain for our healing and health. A healthy organization—whether a marriage, family or a business corporation—is not one with absence of problems, but one that is actively and effectively addressing or healing it problems. Much disease is actually the result of the attempt to avoid the necessary pain of living and the frequent need for repair.[2]

Anger is a powerful force in the growth of a family and the mom who is raising the family. So what does a mother do with the power she discovers?

WHAT'S A MOTHER TO DO?

We offer some cool words to sooth your hot heart, Mom: Feel the emotion, find the source, face the future, forfeit more often, and fight to win!

1. Feel the Emotion

Mom, take a quick anthropological test: Right now as you hold the book, grab a piece of your skin between your index finger and thumb. Got it? Okay, now squeeze. If you find a strong or even subtle inclination to say "Ouch!" you passed the test. You are human. Mom, here is our first bit of advice for you: Be human. If you are human and real, it is very possible your children will still accept you. Most young people want mom, just mom, warts and all. They desire to be parented by a human, not a superhuman. If you won't take our word for it, listen to the truth from the mouth of babes. Fifteen-year-old Pamela said:

My mom should be more personal with me and my brothers. She should talk to us more. She should also be more open. Our relationship is a six because my mom and I never talk or do anything together. I give her the color blue because she's not always the happiest person.

Another fourteen-year-old said:

I would want to tell her everything about me that she doesn't know, but I can't tell her because she would be very mad. Also I'd say "I love you."

One teenager wants to invite her mom into a relationship of real give-and-take; she wants her mom to be human, real, normal. The other wishes to move to the next level of communication, but the fear of mom's blast keeps the truth in the past. Yet, the fourteen-year-old wants to say "I love you, Mom." Real moms, even mad ones, may find real love when they are really human.

Here is a simple way to take an honest look at Hurricane Mom and see just how bad the storm is: check the storm level. As a result of Hurricane Marilyn and a few others blowing through the Western hemisphere, we have learned more about the nature of these powerful foes of weather. A hurricane is defined by five categories:

Category one: Minimal 74-95 miles per hour winds.

Category two: Moderate 96-110 miles per hour winds.

Category three: Extensive 111-130 miles per hour winds

Category four: Extreme 131-155 miles per hour winds.

Category five: Catastrophic winds over 155 miles per hour.

Imagine being the guy out there with the wind sock and the speedometer trying to gauge the windspeed? Only Dorothy and her dog, Toto, could survive devastating winds and live to tell the story. You would think lions and tigers and bears (oh my) would be a push over if you just sailed a two-bedroom farmhouse on the breath of a catastrophic twister.

Mom, it may help to add some humor to your heat. Give your kids the five categories and ask them to name each hurricane level. You can even pick a character from a book, movie, or real life. If you are really brave, invite them to help you see what hurricane is blowing through the house. You may want to set some boundaries on how often or how boldly they forecast your emotions. Imagine hearing, "Mom, I'm feeling a category-four Hurricane Cruella De Ville blowing through the house." You'll get the point in a hurry.

Experienced hurricane survivors offer three bits of advice to handle a storm. First, be prepared. Hurricane season begins in June. When are you, Mom, most likely to be entering a more windy time of your day, your schedule, or your month? Learn the storm patterns, then locate storm shelters. Be prepared, Mom, because you are human.

Second, know the difference between a hurricane watch

and a hurricane warning. A watch means "might." A warning means "will in twenty-four hours." Every seasoned storm survivor keeps a portable radio and/or television accessible when a storm is close by or coming soon. Communication is the lifeline to humanity.

Robin has an agreement with a friend whom she can call anytime when she feels she is ready to explode or her windspeed has topped the 100-mile-per-hour mark. "This friend knows she is my link to safety and sanity when she hears my voice and my one line, 'Attila the Hun has got nothing on me today.' She may be the best resource my kids ever have when Hurricane Robin is ready to strike the Webster coast."

Who do you call when the winds blow and the waves crash? Keeping the communication lines open will help you discern the difference between a watch and a warning.

The last bit of wisdom from hurricane survivors involves what to do after the storm. A few practical bits of guidance are:

- Drive carefully and watch for dangling hot lines.
- Don't go exploring sensitive or dangerous areas.
- Use caution when reentering home.

Mom, the transference of these principles to mother/child relationships is both obvious and exact. Move carefully with your child and watch for the hot spots that still remain. Don't go probing to answer all your questions right after the storm. Finally, after the storm use caution when you reenter the relationship. It is seldom easy to reconcile after a major blowup.

It may take time and caution to reconnect all your services and return to a normal way of life.

Recently our middle daughter, Jamie, has been on a wonderful exploration of her human, emotional makeup. Each night as we say goodnight to her, she will ask us, "How was your day? How were your feelings?" Her sincere, genuine interest shifts us from feeling like parental authorities to feeling like real humans. We have talked with her about various peaks and pits of our days. We have summarized the basic feelings into the following four simple words: glad, sad, mad, bad. Daddy even added "rad" in case there was ever a day or an experience that went beyond glad to a "rad!" level.

In the midst of our shared human experience, our daughter is learning how to understand and identify her emotional makeup. As she hits a hot spot during the day with her siblings, parents, or friends, she is discovering how to say, "I'm a howling hurricane getting near category four. I'm feeling very hurt . . . afraid . . . frustrated." She is learning to feel the emotion and identify the intensity. If she becomes a mom, we hope her response will be humane as she hits those times that will push her anger to the surface.

Mom, once you give yourself room to be human and feel your emotions, you can learn to anticipate your levels of anger and maybe even warn your family. Then, you can move on to the next step: find the source.

2. Find the Source

It is important to understand that anger is the reaction to

the pain of hurt, like the heat from the flame. But anger is not the fuel for the fire. Anger, instead, is the yell in response to the burn. What is at the base, igniting the fuel? In a simple summary, four primary sources cause enough pain to trigger anger in us humans: hurt, fear, frustration, and/or injustice. You find yourself either hurt from a painful source, afraid of pain to come, frustrated that pain won't subside, or unjustly treated by painful neglect of fair (and painless) treatment.

When you are angry, Mom, and you are not sure why, or when you hear your kids say the magic phrase, Mom, quit yelling and chill out! stop and ask yourself a four questions: Am I hurt? Am I afraid? Am I frustrated? Am I experiencing injustice because something is unfair? It is likely you will draw closer to the heat source.[3]

To find the fuel behind the anger, take the quit-and-chill message and twist it to become, "Quiet down and listen." Fifteen-year-old Katie told us about her and her mom. She said:

Our relationship is an eight. We get along well. At times we argue. She doesn't understand what I go through or how I feel. (But besides that, we get along great!) She is the color yellow because she talks a lot.

Katie says life is well for her and her mom, but her mom just doesn't understand. They argue, but of course she is a kid and we already learned, "Fights happen." Possibly Katie's source of anger is her frustration with her mom's lack of listening.

Identifying the source of the storm is a perilous, difficult, brave journey into the eye of the hurricane. It may hurt too much to uncover what you find or you may be tempted to rebury the reason for your hurt, fear, frustration or injustice. On your trip, Mom, always keep your radio near by. Your call for prayer, pastoral guidance, and professional help will be your lifeline to hope and healing.

With an accurate assessment of your emotions and the motives behind them, you can make the next move: face the future.

3. Face the Future

When you face the future, you change your vantage point from the pain of the present to the impact your pain-driven actions will have on the future. Remember the young man Jay who said, *The things my mom yells at me for are not worth ruining my day?* He said, *It just makes me not want to do them.* If the mom took a quick pause—to quiet down and listen to herself and her son—she could open a window, small as it might be, for the future to sneak in. If her son continues to leave his clothes strewn all over his room and the house, mom is ready to hit a category-five hurricane and scream like a mad woman.

Ryan told us earlier his mom's anger *crumbles his heart like a big wave.* True Mom, if you scream loud enough the room may get cleaned, but your child may never return to the ocean again for fear of being destroyed by another large wave. Mom needs to find a way to control her self and influence change in her son. What if she involved the child in the decision with something like:

"Jay, I'm hearing you say my yelling is ruining your day and worse yet, not prompting you to do what I asked you to do in the first place. I don't want hurricanes to keep swamping our house. Here is what I am going to do. The next time I see your clothes lying around, I will give you a hurricane watch. That means a storm has been spotted off our coast.

"The second time I find the clothes scattered on the beaches of our floor, I will give you a hurricane warning. That means a storm is headed our way. The third time my lifeguards find textile remnants out of the drawer, the closet, or the dirty clothes hamper, the storm is going to hit full force. I will do the best I can to not yell, but remember I am human.

"But I will target my emotional energy toward your clothing, not your spirit. I will scoop your clothes up and wash them far on shore, away from our house. In other words, the nearest Salvation Army is going to get your clothes and give them to someone who wants them bad enough to care for them. Jay, when the storm blows, the clothes go. Am I understood, sweetheart? Great, have a wonderful, blue-sky filled day!"

Mom, rise up and check your perspective. Take the helicopter ride, as Doug likes to say, and look down over the lay of the land. Look back from where you have come. Look down on the immediate situation. Then look ahead to the possible outcome. A quick glance to tomorrow may save you a week's worth of clean-up after the storm.

Robin had a recent conversation with one of our daughters, regarding a puppy that may enter our home soon. Of course, our kids desperately want the puppy and they made a monastic pledge to perfection, piety, poverty, and poop detail. We truly believe the surest way to redirect the course of our nation's children is to give them a new puppy every six weeks. We would become a bit of heaven on earth.

Our daughter was negotiating her best, "But, Mommmmmmmm, I promise!" Robin told her we were not ready to say yes. Robin did not say we are saying no, just not yes—yet. Our daughter was angry.

"She quickly retorted to my hate for puppies," Robin said, "my dislike for her requests, and my disinterest in what is best for her well being. I wanted to scream!

"You'd think I had maimed a dog in front of her. It took me a moment to shake off the personal attack and recover from the hurt of her accusations. Then I caught a glimpse of the future. I realized a few things: She will live through this. If not today, someday we will likely get her a puppy. She was disappointed for her loss; she saw me as the cause for her pain and she reacted in anger toward me.

"Somehow I found the strength to quiet down and hear her heart. I let the hot pot cool before I picked up the issue again. We talked through her expectations. I helped her better understand dad's and my response as a maybe but not a no. I let her know I like puppies but the cost and commitment is very serious.

"I knew if I could keep my eyes on the future, as dim as it may have been, I could help my daughter learn a great lesson about one of the most difficult choices in life and one of the greatest sources of pain and anger—delayed gratification. Most pet stores sell puppies to people who can't get past the present. Why do you think they call a major technique in sales, 'the puppy dog'?"

If you are hot and the future looks stormy, take a Time Out. Self-inflict your own discipline weapon. We have had times when we have said to our kids or they've said to us, "Time for Mom (or Dad) to take a Time Out." It's humbling but effective.

Mom, when you're hit by a storm from your child, take a brief spin and spot the future. You may even find yourself ready to take the next step: forfeit more often.

4. Forfeit More Often

We can hear your thoughts, "Wait, my house doesn't have the room for eight new puppies!"

Well, Mom, yes and no. Puppies are wonderful when you merely want to know how much they cost when sitting in the store window. You'll be singing a different tune when you bring Fluffy home. The key question is: How bad will it be? Eventually when we say yes to a dog (it's inevitable), things will get messy for a while. But that's part of the forfeit. Few *yes* answers come without a *no* to something else.

Lets move beyond the canine question, and generalize our statement to moms. What can you forfeit to make the situation less tense, less adversarial? If you are like us, you find yourself conditioned as a parent to say, "No!" as soon as your child says, "Mom, can I?" Or before your child says anything: "But Mom,

I didn't even ask yet." And you respond, "I know, that's why I said *No!* Now go ahead and ask."

Mom, what can you give up to lighten your relationship? Don't give away the store. Perhaps a piece of candy. Or how much will it hurt if the kids spoil their dinner one night? What if you let them wear something different to school or church just one day? What if they stay up late one night just because? Many of the minor squirmishes can be disallowed if mom would be willing to forfeit more often.

Yes, Mom, in a sense you are giving in. But that may not be bad. We call that letting your child grow up. Remember, before you give in, realize you don't give away your child's responsibility for the consequences. When the child gets the choice he or she also receives the price of the decision. Staying up later one night may diffuse the typical, "Oh, Mom. We never get to stay up late argument." Just add, "Okay, you can stay up late. You still have to get up early tomorrow and I am not going to pay an emotional price for your tired bodies. You stay up late, you pay the price. Now, let's have some fun."

A mom who learns how to forfeit more often, especially as the child grows older, is a mother who can turn away the smaller storms that bash the family coast all too often. But of course, Mom, sometimes you don't want to lose. When you feel the necessity, do whatever you can to win.

5. Fight to Win

A fourteen-year-old girl named Karin said:
It's my life, I'll color my hair, and you shouldn't have a say.

Should you have a say, Mom? Recently Robin's sister and brother-in-law encountered the parental hair blues. Our niece came home from college with blue hair. You know, the kind that Giggles the Clown wears at your four-year-old's birthday party. As they were driving to church the next day, one of the family members asked why she didn't color her eyebrows blue as well. She responded:

Are you kidding? That would look so stupid.

Within moments the entire family was in an uproar. Herb had to pull the car over he was laughing so hard. They allowed the choice of their twenty-year-old young adult to bring a moment of laughter to the family and avoid the destructive force of hurricane. What do you think? Should you have a say over your child's hair color? Could you answer yes if she were fourteen but no if she were twenty?

Mom, if you are going to fight, pick your battles carefully. A friend of ours who is a family therapist, Dr. David Rice, has helped many parents, including us, better understand what it means to pick your battles. At a parents seminar hosted by the National Institute of Youth Ministry, Dr. Rice handed out a sheet with a list of topics that may be worth battling over.[4]

Mom, invite your child to the negotiating table and let your child know what areas are worth discussing and what areas you will by no means give up. Highlight these guarded areas and warn your child that you intend to unleash fire power to win those battles. The more serious you are, the stronger your message will be.

Take a look at Dr. Rice's list and ask yourself three questions:

1. Which of these topics are worth fighting over?
2. Will some of the battlegrounds change as my child gets older?
3. What are the direct, clear consequences of a violation of the non-negotiable issues?

Hair Style

Music

Lying to parents

Using drugs or alcohol

Use of time

How the child spends money

Missing curfew by ten minutes

Regular church attendance

Choice of movies to watch

Use of telephone

Attitude

Not doing homework

Joining sports or clubs

Language

Volume of music

Earrings for males

Messy bedroom

Not doing chores

Choice of friends

Missing curfew by sixty minutes

Choice of clothes

Use of car

Manners

Fighting with siblings

Poor grades

Joining family vacations

When you find your keepers, hold them close, speak them loud, and defend them hard. Don't fight to lose. We've heard it said, "Say no as little as possible, as clearly as necessary, and as strong as you can."

You are the mom. You are reestablishing the boundaries we discussed in the previous chapter. You are committing to what's right, true, and valuable. More often than not you will be right, and you will pursue what is best for your child. Let your child know why mom is yelling. You can chill later.

Have you been thinking, *Oh, it's not that bad*? Oh, yes it is. Hearts crushed by moms take years to heal. (You may know that firsthand because of your own relationship with your mother or father.)

Let us offer a warning because of what we hear from some young people. Kids won't stay around forever just because a woman is mom. They may find themselves driven to higher ground with the last message for mom: *I can live without you.*

But there is hope, Mom, even if the island has been badly battered by severe storms. Hard work and recovery may move you back to the previous message from kids, *We get along and we are friends.* You may even be on the receiving end of the next message and the fourth Cheer of the Heart from young people: *You are a fun mom.* We'll let two young girls who have had their fair share of fights with mom offer us hope for tomorrow:

One of these days I'll understand all this madness that's happening between us.
Sheri, fifteen years old

Even though we fight, I hope you know I'll always love you.
Michelle, thirteen years old

We end this chapter with a simple prayer our oldest daughter shared with us:

Now another day is breaking

Sleep was sweet but so was waking.

Dear Lord, I promised you last night never again to sulk or fight.

Such vows are easier to keep when a child is sound asleep.

Today, Oh Lord, for your dear sake, I'll try to keep them when awake.[5]

Dear Mom,

Every time you yell, you close up my heart. You may think I can hear you better, but I can't hear you at all through the noise of your anger. We try to work on our relationship, but neither of us tries enough. Please calm down, or I am going to walk out and I may never come back.

Love,
Your child

CHAPTER 8

Dear Mom,

You're a fun mom!

Thanks,
Your child

YOU'RE A FUN MOM!

My relationship with my mom is a nine. Laughter is generally what keeps us highly rated.

Brad, thirteen years old

My mom is like the color blue, fun and outgoing with everybody.

Shaun, sixteen years old

My mom is the color fuchsia. She's bright and vibrant; sometimes she's just a little bit off, wacky if you will.

Kristin, sixteen years old

Robin's mom has a claim to fame: fanciful tales and legends circle around her. They seem to surface like folklore every time the Glick family gathers beneath the Christmas tree or around the Thanksgiving table. Someone (often one of the three son-in-laws) makes a passing comment about Myrna and the stories commence. Robin's mom is a great sport about the whole thing. (Of course, most of the stories serve to elevate her to star status, especially in the eyes of new family members or friends.)

For instance, like the time she enhanced a spontaneous

water fight by bringing the garden hose into the house, while it was on. She knew how to win a battle! Or the time she put salt in a friend's cup of coffee (enough to choke a horse) and waited to see how graciously he would handle Myrna's bad brew. She has been one to sneak around the house with the kids and a few other (younger) adults, playing tag in the dark of the night. On more than one occasion we've watched her go to the makeshift wrestling mat called the living room floor and do her best to pin a grandchild and tickle like mad.

Then there was the Thanksgiving meal she hosted at her home. Partway into the meal, someone noticed small black specks in the mashed potatoes. Her response was, "Oh, I put pepper in it." "Pepper? You don't put pepper in mashed potatoes," someone else cried. Unless you are Myrna. The "pepper" was soon spotted with legs, and we quickly destroyed the bug-laced part of the meal.

Doug remembers one of his first visits to Robin's parents' house. He was yet to be welcomed into the family as an official member. (Sometimes he wonders if he's ever been officially inaugurated; this may have been the time, however, as far as Myrna was concerned.) The veteran brother-in-laws, Herb and Rich, kicked off the Myrna tales to the delight of the attentive family.

Doug found them quite hilarious so he laughed and chuckled his way through dessert. Mid-stream through a story, Myrna sat next to Doug and asked ever so sweetly, "Doug, do you think the stories are funny?"

"I do," Doug said between bites and bellows. No sooner

had he said that than Myrna pushed his dessert much closer to his face than he cared to wear it. The moment Doug was ready to pounce on her with another piece of pie, she calls time out on account of injury. "My back. Be careful of my back." (She's been through some serious back injuries and surgeries. Of course the back is fine when she is taking a granddaughter to the floor.)

You can bet he thought long and hard before he ever said, "I do" in her presence again.

The icing on the cake were the times Myrna would crawl down the hallway or out back to the window when Robin was a child, trying to go to sleep at night. On more than one occasion, she was greeted by a mother in the dark, a hand in the hallway, or a face plastered against her bedroom window. Her mother's cover was blown a few times by the snickering Robin would hear coming from her as she lay waiting to grab Robin's foot as she went by. Funny, huh? To this day Robin can't go more than five feet in a dark house without memories of mommy anchoring her achilles.

When Robin heard the message of the fourth Cheer of the Heart from kids, You're a fun mom, she smiled. She knew what those kids were talking about. She is doing her best to carry on a legacy of laughter in our own home.

A LEGACY OF LAUGHTER

What is the most fun you ever had with your mom?

Give this question a try at your next social gathering and

see where it goes. Sadly enough, too many people reserve their answer for a small-group encounter or a therapy session.

Let's turn the question around and ask moms: "What is the most fun you've ever had with your child?"

Is it easy to answer the question? You probably spend more time with your kids than your husband so you most likely know what ticks them off and what tickles their funny bones.

Mom, kids love to have fun. They want to experience the upside of life. Listen to what twelve-year-old Jessica has to say about her mom who is the color rose:

She is always so happy and cheerful. She laughs a lot, and believe me, she's always laughing.

When was the last time you laughed? If you can't remember, you are in deep trouble. If you have not laughed with your child, husband, or family together in the current calendar year, you need the ICU. For a family to be healthy, you have to laugh. We recommend laughter on a weekly basis.

Think about the people you have in your home. Surely you have enough normal people doing typical, goofy things to bring about a chuckle or two. We believe if you look for a laugh, you'll find one daily. Life is just too funny.

Each time Doug conducts an annual review with one of his staff members, he asks the person to rate his or her level of fun on the job. No matter how good people are at what they do or how much they get paid, if they don't enjoy the work, the job gets stale quickly.

If you are a working mom, how would you rate your level of fun on the job? If you're in a position of influence, what can you do to bring some fun to the floor? If you do, it will serve a double purpose: the workplace will be more positive, more productive and more personal; and your coworkers will leave happier, which in turn makes for happier daddies and mommies at home. And we all know, "If Mamma ain't happy, ain't nobody happy."

The Emotional Umbilical Cord

Postpartum is a twenty-year condition, longer in some cases. After birth, you still retain the ability to help your child enjoy life. This probably comes as no surprise, but let us reinforce our point with some poignant comments from kids who find life with their mothers very enjoyable:

> *I couldn't live without her.*
> Bonny, twelve years old

> *My mom is the color pink—soft, gentle, considerate. She can also have fun.*
> Tessa, thirteen years old

> *I chose the brightest color there is. Yellow reminds me of the sun. She's always there. Those days the clouds come in, she's always missed.*
> Virginia, fifteen years old

> *My mom is the color yellow-orange. She's like the sun, she shines through dark clouds.*
> Steve, fifteen years old

"But Robin and Doug," you may say, "you just don't know how bad it hurts right now." You may be right. What can you do when you find yourself in the pain we talked about in the last chapter? As the phrase goes, "Laughter is the best medicine."

Finding Fun During the Pain

However fleeting the fun may be, a smile, a story, a joke, a humble laugh at one's self is always healing. The Hebrew proverbs give historic credibility to the power of the healing word of another human. "A cheerful heart is good medicine."[1]

The world of psychology and medicine is pursuing a relatively new field called psychoneuroimmunology or PNI for short.[2] In lay terms, PNI focuses on the power of the human will to live as medicinal treatment for various kinds of ailments including heart disease and cancer. When you want to live, your mind can have a very powerful healing influence on your body.

Most families don't need to understand PNI to find healing. Nor can we oversimplify by stating that a good laugh always makes everything better. But a mom who desires to bring life to a child can go a long way with a laugh, a smile, a positive attitude, and a spirit of hope. Listen to one child who has a mom like this:

> *My mom is the color yellow because yellow is cheerful. My mom is cheerful even though she's often in pain.*
>
> Jennifer, eleven years old

We heard earlier from Jennifer. She is the same eleven-year- old who has attended five mother/daughter conferences with her mom. Now we realize how much more commitment it took from mom to go away with her daughter. Mom, don't let pain plummet the level of life in your family.

Pain is not the only grave digger for fun. A fellow burglar of life is it's cellmate called perfection.

Abandon Perfection When in Pursuit of Fun

Fun is seldom the by-product of perfection. More likely, perfection may rob you of the joy hidden in the cracks of failure. One young person gave his mom the color periwinkle. (Just the name of the color brings life; try saying periwinkle out loud without smiling.) Sixteen-year-old Deborah told us:

My mom is the color periwinkle. Sometimes we don't get along, which would be the blue part, but she can also be springish and happy, when we do get along and have a lot of fun together.

We came across a delightful discovery in our research of fun between moms and their kids. We found an unusual trio of fifteen-year-old girls. There must have been something about women who had babies around 1980 and named them Melissa. Here's what their daughters have to say about them:

Melissa 1: *My mom is friendly, fun, and has a warm spirit.*

Melissa 2: *Always happy and encouraging.*

Melissa 3: *She always sees the bright side of things. She has a positive attitude toward life.*

Mom, drop the perfection and pick up the periwinkle. It may be the beginning of a new season in your life.

When Fun Gets an "F" in Your Child's Book

What do you do if you get the typical teenager statement, "Is this going to be a family thing?" A young woman we quoted earlier adds another insight about kids and their parents by her own self discovery. She said:

I wish I would have recognized earlier that my parents are human beings, and that they could be true friends rather than just annoying voices reminding me to mow the lawn.

Linnsey

One of the fastest ways to let your kids know you are human is to smile and have fun.

Here is another reader participation test for you to try. Right now, put down the book and go find your child. (This is much more fun if your child is not sleeping.) Get his or her attention and simply stand there and smile. Say nothing. Just wait and see what your child does or says.

We bet your kid won't get it. Your child will say something like, "What's up with you? What, Mom, what?" Just laugh and come back to reading the book. (We will forgive you if you engage in fun with your child and delay your return to Dear Mom.) Your child will suggest you ought to start drinking de-caf coffee. Whatever the response, your child will discover your humanity, the important part that likes to enjoy life, sometimes for no apparent reason.

Catch what we write? For *No a-Parent* reason. Mom, if you want to add value to your presence when you are always there, don't always be the parent. Does your child know you are more than an annoying voice, reminding the child of a lawn to be mowed, homework to be done, a bed to be made, clothes to be picked up, stuff to be put away? Mom, we beg you, have some fun. Then it's time to ask, "What's a mother to do?"

WHAT'S A MOTHER TO DO?

How can you initiate a legacy of laughter in your family?

Here are two suggestions: find a fun mentor and live fun.

Finding a Fun Mentor

Two more young women gave us some comments about their moms we want to pass on to you:

My mom is the color yellow. She is full of love and joy. Always happy and brightening the days of everyone she sees.
Amy, twenty years old

She's really nice and funny. She always knows how to make me laugh.
Lisa, fourteen years old

We have two nieces, Lisa and Amy, who are sisters. We are convinced they could offer the same comments about their mom, Laurie. Laurie—Robin's sister—is one of our fun mentors. So is Robin's other sister, Lynette. They both may carry a genetic predisposition from their mother, Myrna. Our kids think Laurie and Lynette are the greatest fun since Barbie® dolls and baseball. Both are hostesses par-excellence when it comes time for holidays. One Thanksgiving feast fit for Kings was followed by the aunts leading the charge for a game of night-time tag with all the nieces and nephews in tow.

When we think of women who cast a lifeline of love and legacy of laughter, Laurie and Lynette come to mind. They are teaching us what it means to live life fully.

We have other fun mentors as well. Another friend named Sandy always seems more concerned about her children's enjoyment than the condition of the carpet. Being a beach fan, she always places greater value on the kids going to the beach than the family car staying spotless and sandless. Our dear friend Kim, has a gracious spirit and charming smile that can turn a peanut butter and jelly sandwich in the backyard into an adventure. Another friend and fun mom, Marti, is one mom you want your kids to know. Her childrens friends love to get invited to the incredible birthday parties Marti throws, like the time she turned her backyard into a pirate's ship for her son's birthday.

Mom, if you are not a fun kind of gal, find a Laurie, a Lynette, a Sandy, a Kim, or a Marti, and imitate them. If you've got a model or a mindset, it is now time to live out your fun.

Live Fun

Here are twenty ways to bring laughter to your relationship with your child.

1. Spend money on your child . . . and your child's friends. One young girl told us:

My mom is really fun. She buys my friends stuff when we go shopping.

We thought we would use this young woman's words to state the obvious: Money brings a smile nine out of ten times.

2. Let your child be the chauffeur. Periodically let your licensed child drive the car, "just because." But wait a moment, mom, don't drive from the passenger side. To this day, many of us adults still dislikes driving a car with one of our parents as a passenger. The backseat driving robs the fun and creates anxiety. If you need to, make it a short trip so your panic button runs a lower risk of being hit too many times.

3. Eat dinner backwards. One night serve dessert first. Say to your family, "Now, remember, I want you to spoil your dinner." You will have them baffled. If they get too full to eat the salad, congratulate them for obeying you and ruining the important part of the meal.

4. Eat dinner in a new location. Serve dinner in front of the television in the family room. Get Chinese food, make everybody take off their shoes, and eat on the floor. Spice up the event with a rented video or the family's favorite TV show (assuming you can find a show you all enjoy.)

Or you could serve dinner in the car and drive around while the family eats. Or eat on the way to a park. Then break for a romp on the playground before you head back to the car for the final course of the evening. (For this, we recommend an easy to eat meal that has a low-spill factor.)

5. Initiate a family awards ceremony. Grant an award to the family member who exhibited the oddest or most hilarious behavior that week. Include yourself and dad in the awards ceremony. During mealtime have the family vote on the silliest act. Award that person an oddball hat that he or she has to wear the rest of the meal. Then honor that kid with either the first shot at dessert or the "privilege" of being the one to clean dishes that night.

6. Videotape family members sleeping. Video cameras can bring all kinds of laughs to the family. One idea is for mom to sneak through the house and collect early morning footage before the beauties face a new day. Show it at the next family gathering. You may find a powerful negotiation tool in your possession.

7. Romance your husband . . . in front of the kids. We don't intend to get PG-13 on this idea, but we picked this up from one of the kids:

My mom stands out like a red rose: beautiful and bold. My mom is

the type of person who knows how to handle her attitude, and be sexy
at the same time. She knows who she is, and is not afraid to show it.

Erika, fifteen years old

Mom, what would happen if you tried to sweep your man off his feet, figuratively speaking of course, in front of the kids? Display affection right to the point where your kids say, "Ohhh, Mom . . . Dad. That's embarrassing."

Young women need to see what it is to be a woman who values love, romance, and affection. Young men need to learn of romance enveloped in respect. Sexuality has more to do with identity and relationship than the act of intercourse. Your husband might go scrambling to get you a dinner on the town and your kids may run for a friend's house.

8. Act silly when you want to scream. This next comment may violate everything we tried to establish in Chapter 6, *We get along,* and the value of boundaries and battlegrounds. If you stay close to our point, you'll get what we mean. Fourteen-year-old Beverly gave her mom the color yellow because . . .

My mom is like a bright sun, always happy and cheerful. She can always make you laugh. When she's covered by a cloud, you can no longer feel her warming rays. I can tell her anything, and when she yells at me I can yell back and we laugh about it.

Our attempt is not to glorify disrespect. You've read how much we honor respect in our family and no child is given room to disregard what we consider vital to our family's well being. What struck us is the thought of a mother and daughter laughing at a time when they wanted to take each other's heads off.

Anger is energy, so if you are careful, you can displace the destructive side of the anger with a burst of humor or laughter. Next time you hit a boiling point, take the lid off and stir in a pinch of laughter or a smidgen of smirk. It may not feel as good as mowing down your kid (or spouse), but it could have better long-term results.

Try yelling in a foreign language, preferably one neither of you understand. Maybe you could stand on your head. (We recommend using a pillow.) You could throw yourself down on the floor, do your best impersonation of a two-year-old tantrum, then ask your child to name the place such a scene occurred. "Right, sweetheart, Wal-Mart!" (Why does every toddler choose a place like Wal-Mart or Target to unsheathe their latest tantrum?)

9. Wack out your wardrobe. Pick a day or a time and wear something completely outrageous. Try it next time you go to the store, attend church, or have carpool duty. Your kids may hate you but the fury is temporary and the memory will last a lifetime. They may someday write a book about you.

10. Go to a public place and watch people. Too many of us rely on the media to make us laugh. Take your child on a date, grab some food, and head down to the nearest airport. Position yourselves in the center and then start eating and watching. Add a twist by trying to guess what these people do for a living or where they are going.

Take turns making up stories about a stranger. Find a new person and add them to the story. Before you know it, you two will be busting up, and the normal travelers will use *you* as a way to find fun in their daily lives.

11. Send your child a telegram in school. Need we say more? Your child will love the attention.

12. Throw a birthday party for your child . . . on the wrong day in the wrong month. Put together a party with the whole package: the cake, ice cream, singing, guests, maybe even a birthday gift. After all is said and done and your kid is still completely confused, end the party with this one statement, "I always wanted to have a child born on this date."

13. Go shopping with $2.19. Give each member of the family the same amount of money and challenge each of them to buy as much as possible with the money. Give them fifteen minutes to shop in the same store at the same time.

14. Deliver surprise gifts to friends or neighbors. Moms can have a great time baking food or making gifts for the sole purpose of brightening up another person's day. You will have an excuse to be with your child and also model what it means to serve other people.

15. Send anonymous cards with money. Pick one name a week and send them a card. Enclose $1 and tell them it is to let them know how valuable they are to you as a friend. Let your child help select the names and write the note on the card.

16. Do a family car rally. Pick ten locations in your neighborhood or community for your family to visit. Any place will do. Add some creativity with public places or spots in which you have to do something or talk to somebody. For example, make one of your stops the local fast-food restaurant where your child has to borrow and wear the hat of the person behind the counter. Throw in a video camera or Polaroid camera to record the event, and you've got years of captured memories. You can even bring in different families and make it a fun competition. (It may work best to split up families.)

17. Put gas in dad's car, incognito. You and your child can conspire to add a few gallons of gas everyday to your husband's car without him knowing. See if you find him saying at the dinner table, "You'll never believe the gas mileage I'm getting lately. It's just incredible!"

18. Go to church. Try attending a different church just to compare to your church. Or if you are not attending a church, try going. We're amazed how few people go to church. The music may be off key and the sermon long, but you'll find a place where the people value a common faith, strive to care for one another, and have a link to joy.

19. Deal the cards. Pull out a deck of good old-fashioned playing cards and share a game. The latest craze in the Webster family is a variation of solitaire, called "Nertz." The kids have the knack so they would just as soon deal a deck as flip on the tube. Other games can offer an attraction to older or younger-aged children.

20. Unplug your television. You decide how long: a week, a month, a generation. The TV is the most subtle, yet powerful anti-fun force ever designed. Unplug the television and reinstate the family.

In light of these possible ideas, ask yourself: When was the last time I saw my family have spontaneous, creative fun just to enjoy each other's company?

Mom, you may just find your child saying what Tamara did:

My mom is fun, exciting, and thrilling to be with. She always tries to make everyone feel at home. My relationship with my mom is a ten. My mom is my inspiration. She brings sunshine to the darkest days.

If a mom doesn't work to loosen or let go, she will not only miss out on the Cheer of the Heart, *You're a fun mom,* she may collect the crushing comment from her child, *I could live without you.* This is an area devoid of fun and filled with pain. It's the focus of the next chapter and the fourth and final Tear of the Heart.

Dear Mom,

You brighten up my life. I have fun when I am with you, and you know how to make me laugh even when the clouds roll in on my life. Even though we have problems, I love being with you.

Love,
Your child

CHAPTER 9

Dear Mom,

I can live without you.

Your child

I CAN LIVE WITHOUT YOU.

My relationship with my mom is a zero. She is bad. I could live without her.

Anonymous, seventeen year old

My mom knows me inside out and is always molding. I know what she means to do but I rebel. Fun often isn't contained within what she wants for me.

Momo, fifteen years old

I don't get along with my mom. I want to live with my dad.

Anonymous, twelve year old

If you spend as much time with kids as we have over the years, you experience or hear stories that seem stranger than fiction.

One of the most incredulous stories is that of a young man named Bobby, as told by M. Scott Peck in *People of the Lie*.[1] During the school year Bobby's grades dropped significantly from a B average. He appeared despondent to his parents and his school administrators and he crashed a stolen car while driving without a license.

At surface level all seemed okay between Bobby and his caring parents. They were his means of transportation for his scout meetings. His mother was active in the local bowling league. They attended church together weekly.

As Dr. M. Scott Peck, the psychiatrist, was to learn, Bobby's greatest concern was how much he hurt his parents. He could tell he hurt them because they yelled at him. Further inquiry unveiled a shattering incident in Bobby's family. His brother had committed suicide eight months earlier. He had shot himself with a .22 caliber rifle. Bobby was unable to articulate his feelings about the suicide, although he spoke of how close he was to his brother. Many adolescents have a difficult time identifying, understanding, and sharing feelings. Bobby was no exception.

Over the course of a conversation, the topic of the prior Christmas, only two months ago, came up. Bobby spoke of requesting a tennis racquet. Instead he had received a gun. A .22 caliber rifle. Bobby's parents had taken the very gun his brother used to kill himself, wrapped it up with a pretty bow, put it under the Christmas tree, and then passed it on to the surviving brother as a gift of love and appreciation.

Bobby's parents were surprised to find out their living son was a high risk for suicide. They just had not thought about it. The mother talked of how difficult it was to take Bobby to his appointment with Dr. Peck because it conflicted with their work schedules. In reference to his dropping grades, the mother simply stated it was a shame because he was such a bright boy. When asked why they would give him that gun as an unsolicited Christmas gift, the parents said they never thought about it. Yet they basically communicated to their child, "Take this and do likewise."

In *People of the Lie*, Dr. Scott Peck, wrote, "Certainly they didn't seem to feel guilty. I didn't feel any empathy for them. I only knew how I felt. I felt repelled by them."[2] When dealing with a child as a patient, he writes, "We usually find the child is not as sick as the parents."[3]

What happens when the very child who once depended on mom for his life never wants to see her again? He has the same feeling as the psychiatrist dealing with Bobby's parents: he feels repelled. Like a spray manufactured to keep blood-sucking insects at bay, repellent keeps us from harm's way.

We found a small but vocal portion of young people sharing with us a very important message:

Mom, I can live without you.

These kids want out and away. In Bobby's brother's case, and very possibly Bobby's, living without mom and dad means suicide. Each choice attempts to accomplish a relational repellent. The most alarming of the options provides irreconcilable finality.

According to young people, the detours in a vital relationship with mom occur when mom over-controls, blocks her heart from hearing the child, and provokes or provides incessant yelling and arguing. This detour eventually leads to a dead end. A detoured child ends up in a suffocating, dark, back alley, and the only way to survive is to leave.

One fourteen-year-old young man named Frank told us what he wants his mom to hear from him:

Shut up, leave me alone, let me do what I want. Why would I say anything to her? We said everything already! Nothing works.

This chapter is lethal. The clear, biting, and emotional words are strong to take. We fear a maternal overdose. To eliminate the chapter will bring relief, but it will also exacerbate the denial striking families who find themselves in pain.

We invite you to take an important walk through the darkest part of a young person's relationship with his or her mom, a world of alienation and abandonment. If the words don't fit your world, celebrate. If they do fit your present or they describe your past, hold on tight. We will listen to children as they speak of life burglars. We will then reach for a light to offer words of hope for a mom or a child lost in a very dark place.

LIFE BURGLARS

What robs young people of a lively relationship with their mothers? We have talked about the consequences of a mom who controls too much, talks too often, listens too little, and yells too loud, but we agree that these aspects can be everyday reality in homes across the land. Raising a child is the most difficult task any human being will every undertake. It is also the most rewarding. What buried treasure is ever found without digging in, getting dirty, and working hard?

One way to end a relationship between a mother and a child is to continue down the road defined by what we call the Tears of the Heart. If kids repeatedly say or act out to mom, *You're always there!*, *I can't tell you anything,* and *Quit yelling and chill out!* to no avail, they lose the energy, courage, and hope to stay close.

Intensity is the fast track to abort the mother/child relationship. Four burglars will break in and steal the very life from a child's heart: blame, hate, denial, and fear.

The Burglar of Blame

The burglar of blame is most often, although not always, an inheritance from a previous generation. A constant battle for mothers is the balance between concern and control, the position on the power bar. A woman who grew up in an environment of over-control may find identity and value when she emulates that control on her own children, even though she fought, despised, and left that control in her own home.

When people cannot control, they can blame. A blamer says, "It is your fault." To the blamer, a problem means a potential failure. When there is a threatening failure, a cause or a *blamee* must be found. That's just the way it was growing up, that is the way it is now. (A non-blamer can say, "We have a problem. What can we do about it?")

When a child grows up in an environment of "It's your fault" she starts believing, "It *is* my fault." When she becomes a mom, she believes life should go as planned (as controlled by the parents), so when life does not go as scheduled, a problem exists. When problems rise, she remembers parents say, "It's your fault." So she does what she saw her parents do. She smells smoke, she sees the clouds roll in, she feels the plane begin to shake, and she grabs the parachute and leaps, leaving the child in the cockpit. Her kids learn to live without a quick-ejection parent and they seek to fly solo.

Another term for the person blamed is *scapegoat*. If a mom can lay the problem on the child ("You know how kids are these days!"), she can alleviate her own pain and avoid losing her image in the family or community. The attention goes to the goat/child as it wanders away from the "good sheep of the family" with all blame saddled on its back.

Moms who read this chapter with identification and pain know exactly what we mean. Their backs reveal the strap marks to prove it.

One mother encountered unbearable pain over the death of her son while she and her husband were away. The call came to them to return home immediately. Upon the parents return they discovered their son had died as a result of a drug-induced accident. In an inebriated stupor, he had attempted to fly off the back of a moving vehicle. The startling loss of her son was excruciating to the mother.

What began as a tragic, painful loss grew into vile bitterness that eventually became stinging blame. The mother considered the driver of the vehicle to be the one most responsible for her son's death. On the fifth anniversary of the boy's suicide, the mother called the driver, a peer of her son's at the time of his death. She asked the driver, now turned young adult, "Do you know what day this is? Five years ago today you took my son's life." Her words bit with venom.

The distraught young man, already devastated over the loss of his friend, found no reason to continue his life. The blame was too heavy to carry. He hung himself.

Blame can steal life. So can hate.

The Burglar of Hate

Many women look to their husbands to replace what they lacked with their fathers, and women look to their children for what they lacked with their mothers. One adult had the courage to share with us what she experienced in her young years with her mom:

My mom is the color grey. She was not exciting, someone to stay away from, never satisfied.

A mom who finds dissatisfaction as the benchmark for her childhood looks back on childhood as a grey, dark, and lifeless world. Hate is the ultimate feeling of revulsion. Hate is the result of extended hurt, abusive violation, and perpetual abandonment. Hate is the final feeling held by a person who cannot control the destructive impact of another human.

Most of us, especially mothers, believe love is the greatest of human capacities. Hate can be equally penetrating, equally influential, equally long lasting. Hate is a person's complete concentration toward one person, one perspective, one past event. Dislike leaves room for change. But sustained dislike without change, lingering anger without resolve, haunting hurt without relief will provoke hate. As hate breaks in, humans run for cover or escape for safety.

Blame and hate can steal life. So can denial.

The Burglar of Denial

Bobby's parents suffered from extreme denial. Blame can be felt, hate can be heard, but denial is often hidden. Add to a family the common encounters raising a child, and a mother can easily find herself saying, "It's no big deal. This is just a phase." She can look at her child's behavior and conclude that all kids do the same. Denial is not believing what you know to be true because the truth is too painful to face.

Denial is also not believing what is true because of your inexperience and youthful naivete. Immaturity says, "This can't be true because I have never done this or seen this happen before. Therefore, it will not happen to me." Too many young women get pregnant from their first sexual encounter because they lived with the denial, "Surely, I won't get pregnant, not me, not here, not my first time."

Blame, hate, and denial can steal life. So can fear.

The Burglar of Fear

"There is nothing to fear but fear itself" is the famous adage. The earthquakes that hit our area are so powerful because of the emotional damage left behind on the humans who ponder the thought: *When will it hit again and how bad will it be this time?* Fear of earthquakes, not the earthquake itself, leaves the inhabitants in shambles. We are amazed how few people die when the ground moves, or the wind blows, or the rivers rise as much as they do. One life lost is a tragedy, but we always marvel that we don't seem to lose thousands upon thousands with every natural disaster.

Unfortunately, we humans have much less control than we would like to believe. As a parent, few feelings drive us like the emotion of fear. Moms lead the way with fears of what may or may not happen to their child. Women can fear their child's failure, their child's death, and even their own loneliness when their child grows up and moves away. Moms can be driven by fear to the point of driving their kids out of their lives.

We've told you about Labor Day 1994 when Jamie had cataract surgery. By the time Labor Day 1995 rolled around, we were ready for a weekend of relaxation. Doug spent the day working on *Dear Mom* and then joined the rest of the family and our neighbor, Kana, for a late dinner. The day was hot and the whole gang could think of nothing better to do than march down to the complex pool for an evening romp in the water. Doug decided to spend a little bit more time at home capturing his thoughts on paper. So Robin and Kana took the three kids to the pool.

Only a few weeks earlier Robin had been praying for the ability to see our oldest daughter, Brookelyn (the one the nurse said had such good lungs) through the accepting, loving, and forgiving eyes of God. Brookelyn's unpredictable behavior seemed to be rubbing Mom the wrong way. Little did she know God would answer her prayer in an unusual way.

Brookelyn and Jamie are good swimmers so they require

little direct supervision. They were splashing around in the shallow end of the pool with two neighbor friends, Pat and Guermo. Robin stood on the steps playing with our three-year-old son, Chase. Kana looked over at the children and noticed Brookelyn laying at the bottom of three feet of water. She mentioned it to Robin who proceeded to ask Jamie to tell her sister not to play like that. Jamie pulled her sister to the surface to pass on mom's warning. Brookelyn was lifeless. Everyone thought she was still playing, until mom saw that her eyes were open and fixed. Robin immediately pulled her out of the pool, yelled for someone to call 911, then began CPR. While she tried to bring life back to our daughter, her insides were screaming, "Please God, don't take her from me. *Please.*"

Doug was pounding away on the computer when Jamie broke into the house yelling, "Daddy. Brookelyn is at the pool and she's not breathing." Every parent's worst nightmare hit our family. A quick call to 911 let Doug know a doctor was on site. The sprint down to the pool seemed to last forever. All along between breaths, Doug kept praying, "Dear Lord, not my Brookelyn. Please, don't take my Brookie."

Brookelyn is a special young girl. She has a contagious giggle that lights up a room. She has a tremendous affinity for athletics, especially swimming. Just a few days prior, Doug worked with her to enhance four different swim strokes. She is a natural in the pool, a fish in human form.

That's why the accident did not make sense. Doug expected to get to the pool and find her sitting in Robin's arms, sobbing slightly, but breathing normally after getting the wind knocked out of her. Instead, she was still lying on the pool deck with three adults huddled around her. Non-responsive. Gurgling noises came from her mouth.

"Is he the doctor?" were Doug's first words to Robin, pointing to the father of one of the boys playing in the pool. His wife was also attending to our daughter. We did not realize he was an obstetrician and she was a labor and delivery nurse—both well-trained in medicine and CPR. They were on the scene in a minute. "How lucky," a nurse told us later. "Divine intervention," Doug added to make sure credit was given where credit was due.

The paramedics, the fire truck, and sheriff arrived only moments later. They found her with vital signs and some return of color, but she was still non-responsive. She moaned and twitched. We kept waiting for the gasp and the coughing up of water and a cry of life. It never happened. We were assured poolside if a swimmer shows any sign of life, the person will recover. Mentally that made sense. Emotionally the words were a poor match with what we saw in our little girl.

In minutes, Brookelyn was on a gurney headed for the ambulance with Robin close behind.

"Mission Hospital. Do you know where that is?" the paramedic asked. "Yes, I do," Doug responded.

With that they were gone. Doug doesn't remember if they used the lights and sirens or not. Funny, we always notice, especially when our son Chase is around. He loves fire trucks. That night, we all loved fire trucks and the emergency crew on them.

We spent a long night in pediatric intensive care, "PEDS ICU," as they call it. Robin remembered her earlier prayer while sitting by Brookelyn. She continued her conversation with God, thanking Him for saving our precious daughter. We could not figure out what had happened. A good swimmer playing in the shallow end with three other kids under the supervision of two adults within fifteen feet, and she nearly drowned. It didn't make sense to us or the medical staff.

Six weeks later, after a battery of tests, the specialists diagnosed epilepsy and a heart disorder. The doctors are still baffled by the presence of the two ailments. We wish we had all the answers, but we don't have that kind of control. If you saw her, you would never known what she has been through. Strength of character and phenomenal attitudes gallop in our children. To say we have become saintly parents is a gross exaggeration. The bond between parent and child is definitely changing. We communicate more deeply. We realize how precious life is and how short it can be. Our kids still do what kids do, the occasional things that drive parents loony, but our perspective has changed. We have become people of deeper faith, especially around water.

We thank the Lord often for blessing us with the gift of Brookelyn for a season longer. She's back on loan to us. So are her sister and brother. We also appreciate the incredible professionals: the paramedics, nurses, doctors, and pediatric specialists. Then there are the friends who rallied with food, compassion, housecleaning, and child care during a stormy season. Without them we would be all alone—in too deep over our heads. Where has God been? He never left. He just showed Himself to be closer than we ever realized.

The thieves of blame, hate, denial, and fear leave people in the barren places of darkness. Eighteen-year-old Jessica said her mom is the color black because . . .

She is filled with negativity.

Whatever the reason, Jessica is left in the dead of night with no light, no love. One young person told us he lives hell on earth. Hell in a common, non-theological understanding is separation from love. In a spiritual sense, it is separation from God.

Hell may be a place of coldness, as much as it is unbearable heat, a spot of abandonment as readily as it is filled with evil crowds, a world devoid of love and rampant with loneliness. The young man spoke vehemently when he said:

*My relationship with my mom is a four. We almost always fight. If I could tell her anything, I would tell her to go to *&#@!*

He seems to be saying:

Mom, I've been living in hell long enough. Now, it's your turn to go there. My life can't be any worse without you, but it could be better.

Unique in this situation, the son wants the mom to leave. He doesn't want to take his life, move out, or run away; he wants mom to go away for eternity. Another fifteen-year-old female feels the same way about her mom. If she could pass on anything to her mom, she told us she would say:

Please run away. Leave me alone.

I CAN LIVE WITHOUT YOU. **207**

Another young person, age twelve, doesn't necessarily want mom to leave, just to stay away. She said:

Mom, get your own life and stay out of mine.

LIFE ON THE BIG SCREEN WITHOUT MOM

Isn't it strange how some successful movies lack the presence of a strong, understanding, friendly, and fun mom? Of course, many of the famous Disney animations are adaptations of well-know childhood books and fairy tales. Think about it for minute. What happened to mom in many of these blockbusters?

- Jasmine of *Aladdin*. She is a motherless, single child whose father is ready to marry her off to the first man worth his stuff, regardless of his love for her.
- Belle of *Beauty and the Beast*. No mom is to be found in this quaint French village home, led by a loony dad. Belle has to find love hidden behind closed doors.
- Ariel of *The Little Mermaid*. There are plenty of females who happen to be sisters but no mom in the deep blue sea. She ventures on land to find fulfillment in a peculiarity of species, a human and a man.
- In *Pocahontas,* the mother of the Indian princess is sorely missed. Pocahontas's memory of her is kept alive by mom's wedding necklace, which she wears around her neck. Still, the mother is gone, with no reason for her absence.

- Cinderella and Snow White. Both of these young woman suffer from a father's inability to choose a worthy wife as stepmom for their daughters.

If asked, these young women may have felt the same way thirteen-year-old Timothy did when he told us about his stepmother:

She is the color red; she is always #@%&! off. Our relationship is a zero. Mom, leave me the "beep" alone! Get out of my life!!!*

How do we bring mom back into the picture? Is there hope for kids who've lost or left their moms, or for moms who've driven their children out of the nest?

Find hope in the words of this young friend:

My mom is the color black because she has a lot of hate in her. I don't have any respect for her, although I do love her. More than anything else, I want to say, "Mom, I love you."

Celeste, age seventeen

What's a mother to do to bring hope back to her home?

WHAT'S A MOTHER TO DO?

Mom, fight the forces of robbery with what may be the most courageous acts of life and love you will ever know: through the power of forgiveness.

Find Forgiveness

A counselor talked with a woman who was struggling with

some very pressing issues in her life, including her husband's infidelity. The wife was struck by the painful presence of her husband's dishonor and disregard for their commitment of marriage. She had every right to be hurt. Her hate for the other woman would be questioned by very few people, especially married women. If she was in denial in the past, it was now displaced by her husband's honest confession of his wrongdoing. Most central to her pain was the fear of "it" happening one more time. "How can I trust him again?" she asked the counselor. She sat immobilized by the life burglars who just broke into her home.

The counselor led with his intuition of what she needed most to recover from a disastrous situation. "You need to ask for forgiveness," he said.

She looked up with tear-stained cheeks and said, "How can I forgive him for what he has done?"

"You did not hear me correctly. You need to ask for forgiveness."

Her mouth dropped open. Her hands rolled up into fists. "Are you kidding? Who has done the wrong here? Am I now to blame for the problem my husband has caused?"

The counselor treaded ever so lightly. "Your husband's action is not the issue right now. He has confessed his wrongdoing. As we speak he is wrestling to gather the courage to say he is sorry and to beg for your mercy. That is not what I am talking about. I am talking about your heart. More than making him pay for what he did, you need to find healing for what you have done and what you have not done, for who you are and who you are not.

"This situation is very real, very painful, and very wrong. But you are carrying pain from the past and living under the pressure of guilt from your mistakes. Until you find pure love that offers acceptance for who you are and forgiveness for who you have been, you will never find healing in your marriage."

The woman stared and the tears flowed. She carried years of pain from her past, her family, her father. She stepped into a marriage, hoping it would finally offer the healing, the love, the forgiveness, or the distraction she needed to remove what she left behind.

This woman must realize that she, too, is at fault; she, too, is wrong; she, too, is human. In the beauty of the Christian doctrine, she is a sinner like every other human. "All have sinned and fall short of the glory of God," the book of Romans states.[4] It is not until we discover the depth of our wrongdoing that we understand the height of the forgiveness.

Often a grown child returns to a parent after the child has a baby of her own to say to a mom or dad, "Wow, the more I parent, the more I understand and appreciate everything you did for me as I grew up. Thank you." With us humans, it is not until we find ourselves in too deep, or our child under the water, that we truly appreciate the precious value of life, air, and land.

A dear friend just lost his wife to cancer. Not long before her death he told us, "Life has taken on a whole new value because of what we have faced with cancer." The presence of pain reveals the value of health. For many who skip through life's peaks and avoid the valleys, the true blessing of rising in the morning and facing a new day gets lost in the hustle. The contrast brings value. It is the sting of sin that unveils the fullness of forgiveness.

Unlike we humans who blame then hate, God does not find a scapegoat. He became one in the death of Jesus Christ on the cross. The base of the Christian doctrine of sin establishes the reality of the human condition in the eyes of God. Human-kind is not divine. We parents are not perfect, holy, flawless, and righteous. We are human. As our children grow older, we become more and more human to them each day. Sometimes they cry out, "I can live without you, because I can't live with you."

Mom, can you truly be forgiven? What if your past is shattered with pain and you don't have it in you to be a new and improved mom? Listen to words of hope from a young friend:

Mom, if you never did another thing, Jesus would still love you.
June, age fourteen

Mom, forgiveness has nothing to do with your actions and everything to do with God's act of love for you. Acknowledge your human inability to right the wrong. Confess your failures to the only One who can hear you. Receive the gift of forgiveness as paid for by the child of your Heavenly Father on a cross of judgment: the gift of love, the gift of life, the gift of "right-ness" between God and a lost mom.

When forgiven by God, a mother can forgive herself. Fourteen-year-old Tony has this very wish for his mother. As you've heard throughout this book kids want to remain close to their moms. Tony and his mom have a relationship of six on the scale because . . .

We argue a lot. We both never give in.

Yet Tony's wish is for an eternal life of closeness to his mom:

If I could say anything to my mom I would tell her, "Come to God so I can be with you in heaven."

Give in, give up, and look up. Then seek the everlasting forgiveness that will bring life back to your family. Start with the simple words, "I'm sorry."

Say "I'm Sorry"

Why is it so difficult to say the three words, *I am sorry?* We all know the answer: those words admit our inability, our problems, and our failures. Some moms think they can't be wrong because they are "mom." Some moms never saw a mom who made mistakes while growing up. But "I am sorry" comes naturally to a person who has already said, "I was wrong. Please forgive me," and who has already heard, "I forgive you."

Robin had a conversation with one of our children who expressed her frustration with a past teacher. She commented on how the teacher yelled at the students. *Whew,* Robin thought to herself, *sounds like she gets the same thing at school as she gets every now and then at home.*

"Sweetheart," Robin told her, "I yell too."

Our daughter responded, "Yeah, but you say you're sorry."

What reinforcement for Robin's determination to say the words I am sorry. Deborah at age sixteen has mastered what most adults will never learn. She said:

Mom, I'm sorry for disappointing you because I love you and never wanted to hurt you.

Mom, it may take a running start, or you may have to begin with very small issues like being late or forgetting a request from the child. Whatever it takes, add the phrase, "I am sorry" to your vocabulary and watch your family come to life. If you are very brave, place it in dialogue with your husband. Work to let your voice, your eyes, and your heart say what your words mean.

When it comes to the woman with the philandering husband, don't misunderstand. Yes, she was betrayed. To make the marriage right, her husband needs to seek her forgiveness and strive to right the wrong he has caused. But imagine the power of love she will bring to the marriage if she were to say, "Honey, I am sorry for the times when I have not been the wife you need, for the times I have been self-absorbed, for the times I have been in this marriage to just get what I needed to get from you. I am sorry."

Ask: "Will You Forgive Me?"

Here is the gold standard test for you to consider: When

was the last time you sincerely said, "I am sorry" or "Will you forgive me?" The frequency and intensity of the use of these phrases will say more about your role as a mom than any other factor.

Mom, much like the communication of the heart we covered earlier, forgiveness cannot be forged. It has to be offered. Your child may forgive you, especially if you were very sincere in your apology. Your child may not forgive you for a while. Or, your child may never forgive you. Until you seek forgiveness, you'll never know which option a child will choose.

When you ask forgiveness from someone you place yourself under the person. You understand them and you empower them. Asking forgiveness gives the child the upper hand and you assume the position of a humble servant.

Offer: "I Forgive You"

To complete the reconciliation, you may need to be ready to deliver a treasured gift in your relationship with your child. Thirteen-year-old Danielle knows what we mean. She gives her mom the color white because . . .

She's forgiving.

Forgiveness is the prized arrow in every parent's quiver. Kids are kids and they find ways everyday to prove it. Their job is to experiment with life. Sometimes they fail. Okay, they fail quite often. They give each of us parents a repetitive opportunity to practice sharing with them the forgiveness we find in the eyes of a loving God with our kids. Nothing, and we repeat nothing, will reinstate and revive a relationship like forgiveness. "I love you" says we share wonderful things together, but it is often motivated by what we get from the other person. "I forgive you" says "I love you *still*."

A woman recently shared her mom story with us. On the very day after her parents got a divorce, her dad married another woman. Her mother did not even have the time to clean out all her personal belongings before the new mom was in the house, hanging clothes in the closet and sleeping in her bed. The bitterness was blinding.

As years passed and hate built, the woman's mother died. Not long after, her father became sick. Time at the hospital put the daughter in constant contact with her stepmother. The woman had come to know a Lord who would rather die than live without her. She turned her bitter, blame-ridden, hate-filled heart over to this great surgeon. She found forgiveness. She found strength. She found new life. She found a love she could now extend to her stepmom:

"One day I found myself sitting next to my stepmother at the grave site. We were both exhausted from the turmoil surrounding a man we loved so dearly. I peered at this woman I had grown to hate over the years and I saw a simple, frail lady looking for love. I grasped her hand and with a tenderness that surprised myself, I spoke to her.

"'My dad just died and my mom is no longer here with me. Madeline, I don't have a mom anymore. Will you be my mother?'

"She cried. She hugged me and then offered to me what we both needed for so many years."

This woman's courageous act of forgiveness brought life to a dying situation.

Mom, if you hear the words, *I can live without you,* do three things:

Take it seriously.

Take it to God.

Take the love you find from God and bring it back to your child.

This is no simple formula, nor is it an easy task. But you have no other option unless you want to spend the rest of your life living a hell on earth and dying a slow death. With the pressures facing kids these days, their death may be neither slow nor figurative. If you do what a mother can do because of what God has done, you may find yourself on the receiving end of what a seventeen-year-old shared with us:

I appreciate so much my mom's love and hugs, her smile, patience, and unconditional forgiveness.

If you stick it out as a mom, you will experience what we heard from kids in the final message, *I love you and I appreciate everything you've done for me.*

Join us in the next chapter for a party for you, Mom. For some moms, it will be a surprise party. Of course, we can't speak on behalf of your child, but we can declare the heartsong of hundreds of voices who want to make you, Mom, the life of the party for you are the one who brought the party to life.

Dear Mom,

   *I can't keep living like
this. My life with you isn't a
life at all, and I can find life
without you. I want to stay
close to you and I want to
love you, but you have to stop
pushing me away. More than
a hate for you, I hate how far
apart we are. I wish we were
close again.*

Love,
Your child

PART THREE

THE
CELEBRATION OF
MOM

WHAT KIDS SAY . . .

"Thank you, Mom. You do so much for me"

"Mom, you're number one."

"I'm so lucky to have you as my mom."

WHAT KIDS MEAN . . .

"Mom, you are loved and worthy of praise and thanks."

WHAT KIDS NEED . . .

"Moms!"

CHAPTER 10

Dear Mom,

I love you and I
appreciate everything
you've done for me.

Your child

MOM, I LOVE YOU AND I APPRECIATE EVERY-THING YOU'VE DONE FOR ME.

You are the greatest mom a guy could ever have. No one could ever, ever take your place in my heart.

Marvin, eighteen years old

Even though it's hard for me to come out and say it, I really love you and thank you for all you have done for me.

Ragan, fifteen years old

I love you, but when words are said so much they lose their zing, so I would rather clean my room before you asked, or give you flowers on a really bad day, or just for once see things your way.

Kristin, sixteen years old

This chapter is the Mother's Day of this book. So many young people wanted to let us know how important mom is to them we decided to end with these cheerful messages from the kids. We call it "The Celebration of Mom" because your child wants you to know:

Mom, I love you and I appreciate everything you've done for me.

The sacrificial labor of love that began months before your child ever arrived is coming to a head with this proclamation from your child: "You are loved, Mom." And a second message was woven into the "I love you" message: Young people are grateful for mom because she *does* so much for them. Kid after kid was compelled to let us know their mom is not just lovable, she is also worthy of praise and thanks. Mom is the workhorse for the clan, the engine behind the little child that could, and many times the soul of the family. Sure, many dads are loved and most of them are diligent providers, but in many families, mom gets the job done. This is a tribute to mom.

Brian Forth is one young athlete who can testify to the presence of mom and her influence on his athletic success. In a recent article in the local newspaper, Brian's reputation as one of Orange County, California's leading pass receivers put him at the top of many prep sports admirers.[1] The article caught our attention for two reasons: First, Brian gives a powerful tribute to his mother. Secondly, Brian attends Esperanza High School in Anaheim, California, Doug's alma mater.

What mattered most to Brian was the presence of his mom, Alice, rooting for him at every game. "She really enjoyed the games a lot and watching me play," Brian said about his mom. He now speaks in past tense about his mother. In April, 1994 Brian's mom lost the game to the opponent of cancer. What did her death do to her son? In the eyes of his head coach, his mom's passing may have increased his maturity and ability to handle life.

His coach said, "His leadership is the biggest thing for us.

The other kids look to him when the going gets tough." Much like the times Brian looked to his mom in the stands or across the kitchen table, Brian's teammates and peers now reach to him to find the strength to continue on in the game. Brian's mom left a legacy of love and influence her son Brian is now spreading across the Aztec campus.

Mom, your time with your child is precious. One wise young person named Maria shared with us her love for her mom and the reality of one day losing her. She wasted no time to pass on a tribute:

Mom, thanks for always being there for me. One of these days God is going to take you away from me and I will be left alone in the darkness, with no guidance. Therefore I would like to take the time to tell you what I usually don't say . . . te amo (I love you).

Maria is not alone. We've gathered a few other comments from kids who care a great deal about their moms:

I'm so lucky to have you as my mom! You're my life and I love you so very, very much.
Virginia, fifteen years old

Thanks for being a great mom. I love you. I couldn't ask for anything else.
Chris, fourteen years old

One young man thinks his mom may doubt his love for her based on the track record of their communication lines, but he still loves her dearly. Sixteen-year-old Mike says:

Even though I bicker and annoy you, deep down I really do love you.

Beyond his awareness of the annoyance he is to his mom, he possesses a greater awareness: his love for his mom. To bicker is superficial; to love is substantial. Annoyance is shallow; love is deep. Mike is fortunate to have such a loving mom in his life. And Mike is not alone.

A PERSONAL EXAMPLE OF LOVE

As critiqued by Doug's professional expertise and validated by his personal experience, his three children are incredibly fortunate to have Robin as their mother.

"Truly one of my greatest joys in life is watching Robin live out a deep love and value for her children. When it comes to being a mom and doing the work of motherhood, Robin is one of the best I have ever seen.

"When struck by the likes of surgeries, bike accidents, mean kids, dark nights, outdoor noises, EEGs, EKGs, and MRI tests, new classes, sick tummies, Robin is unbelievably tender and compassionate, as well as composed.

"Robin's presence with her children is balanced by her continual effort to give them the room they need to one day soar on their own. I observe her pushing our kids toward the edge of the nest with gentle but direct words, 'You can fly. I know you can. Now, leap and flap your wings with all your might.'

"Robin is not for lack of opportunities and dreams of her own. Each week for five years she has gathered in front of hundreds of women to share her experiences and insights with young moms who are anxious to fly close to her pattern. Never have I heard women speak of Robin's arrogance. Her humility and transparency cast a contagious air about her that attracted me to her in the first place. When not speaking and mentoring, Robin can sing like her namesake, enabling a sanctuary of people to climb above daily, earthly trials and soar in the heavens. A dream for a singing and speaking career has never taken place of her commitment to her children and their dad. All the while she cares for her children, she keeps her eyes on the Creator.

"Don't misread my praise. There are times when Robin wants to quit the job she began ten years ago. Catch our house at the right time and you will find the volume high enough to break glass. A running joke between Robin and her dear friend Kim Carpenter is summarized in one phrase: When one of them feels that they just did something to forever ruin the psyche of their child, they will say, 'Put another quarter in the therapy savings jar.'

"Robin has times when she wants to garage sale the kids, sub-lease them out, or send them to a foreign country and pay a world relief agency like Compassion or World Vision $24 a month to feed, clothe, and educate them while they live in Quito, Ecuador. Knowing Robin, she'll write periodically and visit annually.

"Think about it: We've been married nearly fourteen years and we have three kids and a dog. You read between the lines. Life is very normal around the Webster house and Robin is not competing for saint of the year. Simply put, she is a

dedicated mom who works very hard to succeed at her job.
And she does."

Fortunately for young children and our society in general,
Robin is in the distinguished company of countless moms who
are worthy of the status of a national treasure. We have heard
from hundreds of young people who shower their moms with
love. One young woman named Kim paints a colorful picture
of her mom:

*My mom is the color pink because pink is a mix of red and white.
Red equals love; white equals pure. I love you, Mom, and I thank
you for all you've done for me.*

MOM, I APPRECIATE EVERYTHING YOU'VE DONE FOR ME.

You may get the point but we want to take a few pages to
really rub it in. Mom, your child loves you and your child wants
to thank you for everything you have done and continue to
do. Here are three guys who want to deliver a tribute of thanks
to mom. Consider them the mom color guard, offering a
twenty-one gun salute:

I do appreciate what you've done in my life.
Dan, age thirteen

I would tell you plain and simple, "You did a good job."
Chris, age fifteen

I am very proud of you, Mom.
Josh, age seventeen

In case you are still not convinced, we want to put you in a mom lineup, turn the spotlight on, and bless you with a bouquet of praise. For some, like twelve-year-old Nicole, it does not matter how many moms crowd the stage; she stands in ovation for one. She says:

If I could pick any mom, I would pick her.

So if you will, Mom, please stand and face the audience as we pass to you six reasons young people offer thanks to mom. We will go silent for a moment so you can absorb the applause.

1. Thank you, Mom, for being there with me.

I love you. Even though I don't show it a lot. I appreciate what you do for me. Thank you for coming out and watching every game.
Michael, sixteen years old

Dark blue is my favorite color, and you are my favorite person to be with. I love you very much. I will never stop.
Richard, thirteen years old

2. Thank you, Mom, for loving me.

Mom, you are the color red because you are really loving and, okay, your red hair.
Nicole, twelve years old

I can rant and rave to you, Mom, and you still love me.
Krisanna, seventeen year old

3. Thank you, Mom, for forgiving me.

I love you for being there through thick or thin.
Andy, fourteen years old

Thank you for helping me through the years.
Michael, thirteen years old

4. Thank you, Mom, for being an example to me.

You are my role model, my inspiration.
Jeanette, eighteen years old

You are the color purple because purple is royalty. I look up to you all the time. To me you are a queen.
Brenna, fifteen years old

5. Thank you, Mom, for sustaining me.

You are what keeps me going. You make me strive to get good grades.
Saran, fourteen years old

I love you! You are the "wind beneath my wings." That song is you, Mom!
Chasity, twenty one years old

6. Thank you, Mom, for serving me.

I appreciate all the time and extra things you do for me. You always go out of your way to please your family. Thanks, I love you!

Tim, nineteen years old

Thank you for all the times I have forgotten to thank you for all the many things you have done selflessly.

Jambolya, twelve years old

The reasons for praise and thanks are very clear, but far from exhaustive. We would run out of pages if we were to list all the ways kids offered thanks to their moms.

Young Ryan had a sense of humor when he offered this comment:

Mom, you raised me. I at least deserve to buy you a steak.

Mom, how would you like your steak cooked? Medium? We bet Ryan would be willing to drive you to the restaurant and open the door for you. You are worth the chivalry.

A young man named Daniel Sahs did more than buy a filet for his mom. He gave her life with his very own. Daniel, a nineteen-year-old engineering student in Wauwatosa, Wisconsin was playing volleyball when he suffered a fatal heart attack. His forty-four year-old mother, Anne, was undergoing dialysis three times a week as she waited her turn on a donor waiting list. She received her son's kidney in an emergency transplant, and she was reported in good condition after the surgery. The transplant took place only days before Mother's Day, 1995.

Scott, a youth only two years younger than Daniel, offers similar words when he thinks of his mother:

My mom is the color red, the color of love, the color of blood, part of what we are. This is my mom.

Children know mom is not just where they come from, but also part of who they are. Ryan wants to celebrate the gift of love he received from his mom. Daniel was able to give back to his mom the life she gave him. Scott and hundreds of others want to pay a tribute of love and thanks to their mothers. William James, once said, "The deepest principle in human nature is the craving to be appreciated."[2]

If his observation about appreciation is true, Mom, welcome to a meal fit for queens.

May these testimonies meet a craving deep in your heart. Mother's Day is only one day a year, but the words of appreciation and love are genuine and heartfelt. On behalf of a thousand young people, here's to a celebration to you, mom:

Mom, I love you and I appreciate everything you've done for me.

> *Dear Mom,*
>
> *I cannot begin to thank you for the many things you have done for me over the years. I really do appreciate you, even though there are times when I forget to tell you. More than anything, Mom, I want you to know I am glad you are my mom, and I love you!*
>
> *Love,*
> *Your child*

APPENDIX A

Some people have asked, "How do the messages of kids for moms and dads you found in *Dear Mom* and *Dear Dad* compare to each other? Here are a few key thoughts we discovered after we listened to 2,500 young people talk about dads and moms. Of course, these are thoughtful observations, not hard and fast conclusions or diagnoses.

- Kids are asking Dad to be around more and Mom to give more room. Young people do have issues of trust with Dad, and some want to spend more time with Mom; however, when parents are at fault in their kids' eyes, Mom is present too much, and Dad is absent too often.

- Mom is the doer of the family, and Dad is the provider. We get the sense that Mom is the engine for most families, and Dad is the fuel.

- Mom is the mayor or chief administrator running the family. Dad is often the sheriff, bringing law and order to town. Moms manage daily issues, and dads face the big battles.

- On the one to ten rating (ten being highest), moms

averaged 8.03, and dads got a 6.93 rating from kids. Sixteen percent of dads and 24 percent of moms received a ten from their child. Girls ranked dads lower than boys ranked dads (6.83 vs. 7.07), yet the girls ranked moms higher than boys ranked moms (8.07 vs. 7.98). According to the young people, dads need to concentrate more energy on the daughters to raise the curve.

- Young people give moms red, yellow, and blue as the top three colors, whereas dads get blue, red, and white as the first three picks when kids paint them a color.

- Moms experience a greater quantity of conflict with their kids than dads, but they also seem to lace the family with more fun and life than dads.

- Kids appear to fight more with their moms than with their dads, but the existence of anger between dads and their kids is a real concern for some young people. When moms lose control, they yell more often than dads. When dads lose control, they get mad and let their kids have it with actions or consequences.

- The majority of young people, regardless of bad child/parent press, are grateful for their moms and dads. They want to thank Mom for what she has done for them, and they want to remind Dad that he means a great deal to them.

APPENDIX B

Books for moms

Beside Every Great Dad by Nancy Swihart and Ken Canfield, Tyndale, 1993

Every Day Miracles by Dale Hanson Bourke, Word, 1989

NIV Women's Devotional Bible, Zondervan, 1990

Parenting: Questions Women Ask by Gail MacDonald, Karen Mains and Cathy Peel, Multnomah, 1992

The Myth of the Perfect Mother by Kimberly Converse and Richard Hagstrom, Harvest House, 1993

What Every Mom Needs by Elisa Morgan and Carol Kuykendall, HarperCollins/Zondervan, 1995

Books on kids, families and marriage

Drug Proof Your Kids by Jim Burns and Stephen Arterburn, Gospel Light, 1995

The Future of the American Family by George Barna, Moody, 1993

Leaving the Light on by Gary Smalley and John Trent, Ph.D., Multnomah, 1994

Love Is a Decision by Gary Smalley and John Trent, Word, 1989

Our Journey Home by Gary Bauer, Word, 1992

Parenting Isn't for Cowards by Dr. James Dobson, Word, 1987

Parent Power by John Rosemond, Andrews & McMeel, 1990

Parenting with Love and Logic by Foster Cline and Jim Fay, NavPress, 1990

Radical Love (Love, Sex, and Dating) by Jim Burns, Gospel Light, 1995

Right from Wrong by Josh McDowell and Bob Hostetler, Word, 1994

Six Point Plan for Raising Happy, Healthy Children by John Rosemond, Andrews & McMeel, 1989

Personality inventories

Myers Briggs Type Indicator by Consulting Psychologists Press, Inc., Palo Alto, CA.

Taylor Johnson Temperament Analysis by Psychological Publications, Los Angeles, CA.

Organization Resources for Moms

Focus on the Family, 8655 Explorer Dr., Colorado Springs, CO, (719) 531-3400

Home by Choice, Inc., P.O. Box 103, Vienna, VA, 22183

MOPS, 1311 South Clarkson, Denver, CO, 80210, (303) 733-5353

Mothers First, Washington, D.C., (703) 827-5922

Minirth Meier New Life Treatment Centers, Dallas, TX,
 1-800-NEW-LIFE
The National Institute of Youth Ministry, 940 Calle Amanecer,
 Suite G, San Clemente, CA, (714) 498-4418
Women of Influence, P.O. Box 6000, Colorado Springs, CO,
 80934

APPENDIX C

Ceremony of Covenant to a Child

A marriage is a public ceremony proclaiming the betrothed spouses' personal feelings toward each other. A member of the clergy leads the couple through vows of commitment before God and surrounding witnesses.

Here's an idea. Would you be willing to go public with your commitment to *your child* before God and surrounding witnesses? Since we do not know of any similar ceremony on behalf of children, we hereby want to institute the Ceremony of Covenant to a Child.

As impressive as the title sounds, the event can be as simple or as elaborate as you wish. The central issue is a parent's commitment to his or her child until the child reaches the age of adulthood, usually eighteen to twenty-one years of age. It's mom and/or dad's way to say, "I'll always be there for you."

What would the Ceremony of Covenant to a Child (or CCC for short) look like? Let us take a stab at the idea.

The appropriate age: We suggest nine years of age or older. A child could participate sooner, but we believe the significance of the commitment is stronger when the child understands what is taking place. In essence, Mom, you are making a public commitment for nine years until the child reaches an age of adulthood.

The appropriate place: Wherever best suits your intent: your living room with a few friends or family members, or at someone else's home to give the event more than just a family feel. Or you may even want to consider a church, which might give added sanctity and value to the event. Your church may be a little confused trying to arrange a weddinglike ceremony for a nine-year-old, but we believe most churches will champion the idea once they understand it.

A token of remembrance: Many families today are asking their children to make a commitment to sexual purity until they are married. Often the parents give the child a ring, necklace, or some other token to symbolize the child's desire for faithfulness and fidelity. A similar token might be used for the covenant ceremony.

An appropriate program: As a minister who has performed many marriages over the years, Doug looked into his marriage file to find an appropriate order of service for the ceremony. Here's a possible format with vows you can use in your own CCC:

> *Seating of the guests*
> Entrance of the child and parents
> Welcome to guests and general prayer of invitation and
>   blessing
> Charge: a few words of exhortation from a minister, friend,
>   or parent
> Scripture reading
> Vows

I (parent) commit to you (child) as your parent before God, our families and friends to promise to love, honor, respect, and protect you in sickness and in health, in plenty and in want, in joy and in sorrow, as long as we both shall live.

I promise to recognize the abilities and gifts God has given you and encourage you to use them to His greatest possible glory.

I promise to work at being the best father/mother I can be for you.

I promise to give you room and support to grow up in the ways best for you.

I promise to remain faithful and sexually pure to my spouse as an example and commitment to you.

Next, adapt the words to fit the child's perspective.

Thirdly, consider doing as Doug does when he officiates at a wedding. He changes the vows to ask the congregation for a commitment to support the couple, their marriage, and their well-being. If they agree, they say in unison, "I do."

Exchange of token while repeating these words: "I give you this ring as a token of my constant faith and growing love."

Prayer of blessing on the child

Pronouncement: I do hereby pronounce you a family committed to one another.

Kiss/hug/handshake/high five

Other details you might want to consider:

Music. Taped or performed music can be used throughout the ceremony to bring special meaning.

Invitations. You could create a guest list, select pretty invitations, and mail them to your guest list. Be careful to specify your intent with gifts.

Involvement. Mom, don't make this your party! Involve your child as much as possible. Remember, it is a family commitment to one another. Have your child address envelopes, prepare the food, decorate the living room. If you can, drop your expectations of others and work to make the time special for you and your child.

Concerning boys. The ceremony will undoubtedly be different for a nine-year-old boy than it will for daughters, older or younger. Be creative in ways you can involve your son, affirm his masculinity, and still present him with a commitment from you.

A word of caution. Some people may not understand what you are trying to accomplish. Expect funny or probing questions, subtle or not so subtle criticisms, or flat-out confusion. Communicate your purpose for the ceremony and ask your friends to consider attending because of what they mean to you.

We have a request if you actually carry out a ceremony. Please drop us a line in care of our publisher, Thomas Nelson, 501 Nelson Place, Nashville, TN 37214. We'd love to hear about your event so we can pass on your insights and suggestions to other parents.

N O T E S

Chapter 1

1. Lee Iacocca with William Novak, *Iacocca, An Autobiography* (New York: Bantam Books, 1984), 7.
2. Ibid.

Chapter 2

1. Kinney Littlefield, "She-TV," *OC Register*, 7 May 1995, 1.
2. Linnsey Workman, "Just 40 more days till we part our ways," SVN/RSM News, 28 April 1995
3. Doug Webster, *Dear Dad*, (Nashville: Thomas Nelson, 1995), 99–125.
4. Psalm 18:2.
5. Barbara Bush is quoted by *Current Thoughts and Trends*, January 1995, page 3, as found in *Home Life*, December 1994.

Chapter 4

1. Proverbs 20:5, *The Student Bible*, New International Version (Grand Rapids, MI: Zondervan, 1983).

Chapter 5

1. Gary Smalley and John Trent, *Love Is a Decision*, (Dallas: Word, 1989).

Chapter 6

1. John 15:13.

Chapter 7

1. Richard M. Nixon, *1999*, (New York: Pocket Books, 1989), 66.
2. M. Scott Peck, *A World Waiting to Be Born*, (New York: Bantam Books, 1993) 10 and 11.
3. We suggest two helpful books, *Making Anger Your Ally* by Neil Clark Warren and *The Angry Man* by Stephen Arterburn.
4. Dr. David Rice has been a guest speaker at numerous NIYM training events. For more information on his work and writings, contact him at (714) 552-0275.

5.   Ogden Nash, *Prayers for Children*, 1902-1971, 10.

Chapter 8

1.   Proverbs 17:22.
2.   Writings by Norman Cousins are the most common mainstream materials for laypeople to understand the discoveries of PNI. See his works *Head First, A Biology of Hope*, and *An Anatomy of an Illness*.

Chapter 9

1.   M. Scott Peck, *People of the Lie*, (New York: Touchstone, 1983), 47ff.
2.   Ibid., 57 and 58.
3.   Ibid., 59.
4.   Romans 3:23.

Chapter 10

1.   Steve Fryer, "Forever Mother's Day," *The Orange County Register*, 19 October 1995, sports section, 1.

About Dear Dad
by Doug Webster

Dear Dad is for every father who wants to better understand his child. Its touching and inspirational messages will enable you to draw closer to your child by discovering what he or she thinks, feels, and needs.

"I'm not coming to you as an expert on fatherhood. I don't have a Ph.D. in 'Daddiology.' But I have credibility—I'm a dad. I've learned a lot I want to pass on to you. Maybe as I share some of the insights I've gained, you'll discover an idea or a practical tool to help you draw closer to your own children."

While addressing important issues in your child's life such as acceptance, self-esteem, forgiveness, and approval, Dear Dad shines a light on the eleven key messages from kids to their dads: "I love you," "Forgive me," "Accept me," and "Trust me," are among a few.

This heartfelt book will open your eyes and your heart to what is going on inside your children . . . what they are saying, what they mean, and what they need—no matter what their ages.

"Fathers, let's listen to our children. This book will stir your hearts."
–Bill McCartney
   Founder, Promise Keepers
   Former Coach, University of Colorado